DATE DUE

DEVELOPING COUNTRIES AND N.A.T.O.

ATLANTIC SERIES

A COLLECTION OF STUDIES ON SUBJECTS

RELATED TO THE NORTH ATLANTIC TREATY ORGANIZATION

DEVELOPING COUNTRIES AND N.A.T.O.

STRATEGIC ECONOMIC IMPORTANCE
OF THE DEVELOPING COUNTRIES FOR N.A.T.O.

by

M. W. J. M. BROEKMEIJER

Dr. econ. Rotterdam

A. W. SYTHOFF – LEYDEN
1963

*The research for this publication
was made possible through the granting of a N.A.T.O. award.*

PREFACE

The preparation of this little book was made possible thanks to a generous grant awarded to me by the North Atlantic Treaty Organization. I hope that it may assist in promoting a realistic appreciation of the worldwide problem of the development of the backward countries, and at the same time contribute towards a better understanding of the strategic, economic and political importance of the developing free world for the Atlantic Community.

I wish to acknowledge my gratitude to all the authorities of the N.A.T.O. member countries who supplied the statistical material used in this study.

I am also grateful to the Economic Information Service in The Hague, and to all the other institutes in the Netherlands, which gave me much valuable assistance.

Finally, I should like to mention that the content of this book has been greatly enriched by the work of my assistant Drs. C. J. Brakel, and by discussions of the wider aspects of the subject with authorities and experts in various countries.

Voorburg, February 1963.   M. W. J. M. BROEKMEIJER

5

CONTENTS

CHAPTER I

INTRODUCTION

Voltaire once wrote "On entre en guerre, en entrant dans le monde"[1], by which he wanted to imply that everybody is living in time of war from the very moment he is born. How true his statement was, is proved by a study made by the Norwegian Academy of Sciences. This investigation showed that during the 6,560 years of known and recorded history of human existence only 292 years have been free from the clash of arms.[2] No less than 14,531 conflicts—large and small—have occurred during this period of "human civilization" and roughly some 3.6 milliard persons have been slain—not to speak of the multiple of this number that have been wounded or crippled for the rest of their lives. Nobody will deny that this is a very serious and depressing record. Do we really conclude from these figures, that any effort to keep peace has no sense at all and that we are absolutely unable to prevent war? Thousands of books have been written, giving all the details of these numerous conflicts and wars. They tell us everything of the war heroes and of the mistakes that were made during those wars by the military and political leaders. All that has been written may be very interesting from a historical point of view. We learn that aggressors started war, justifying aggression on religious, psychological, economic or any other grounds. All these aggressors had the firm idea that their forces were superior and that surprise would be in their favour, so that they did not take too much risk by starting a war.

It is for this reason regrettable that we lack any historic records of all those cases where aggression did not take place in consequence of a balance of power resulting in too great a risk for the aggressor in starting war. Every aggressor will only risk war when he knows that he gets a profit out of his military action and thus will be able to achieve the political aim for which he started a war. Nicolson wrote: "Through centuries of conflict the Europeans had come to learn that war in almost all cases was contrived with the expectation of victory and that such an expectation is diminished under a system of balanced forces which renders victory difficult if not uncertain".[3]

1. Voltaire, Épitres XXXIV.
2. R. Hargreaves, The Hydra-Head of War, Military Review, March 1961.
3. H. Nicolson, Peace-making, p. 192.

I am deeply convinced that there are enough examples in history proving that war did not break out through the firm conviction that war could not pay. When there exists a balance of power between nations in conflict with each other, the outcome of war will be very doubtful and therefore not desirable. The same way of reasoning we meet in a statement by Bismarck, who declared that the fear of a modern war and the incertitude of the outcome of war would have more influence on peace-keeping than any charter to ward off an armed conflict. How many of the 14,531 conflicts mentioned above, would never have taken place if the aggressive monarchs, dictators or governments had known beforehand that the nations they were threatening possessed a military power of such a strength that the outcome of war was really doubtful and that these nations would defend themselves till the bitter end.

The number of statesmen underestimating the threat of war is high. Some feared—for political reasons—to tell the people that the political situation was getting worse and therefore did not plead for an increase of the defence budget. Others underestimated the military strength of the aggressive nation. On July 23, 1914, Lloyd George, Chancellor of the Exchequer, advised the Houses of Parliament to reduce the defence budget, claiming that the relations between Germany and France had never been so good as at that moment.

Furthermore he said: "They begin to realize that they can co-operate for common ends, that the points of co-operation are more numerous and more important than the points of possible controversy. All that is to the good."[4] Twelve days after this reassuring speech by Lloyd George, the First World War started!

War is a feature of human behaviour. The world has always lived under the threat of death and war. It is astounding, when looking at the cruelty and suffering imposed by war upon mankind, that creatures out of the same mould have not yet found the way to reach world peace. A sound and widespread investigation of world history may prove that lack of balance of military power, or the firm belief that there existed an imbalance of power, too often resulted in stimulating the controversy between conflicting nations and finally invited the strongest power to take aggressive action. Weakness and hatred (in the latter case through mass psychology using the worst motives) in popular masses have long been, in one form or another, one of the greatest perils to peace. This is also true of today!

Hesitation of the political leaders to take in time the required defence measures and to convince the threatening nation that war will be

4. Hansard, Chapter 65, column 727 and 728.

fought with all weapons, including the most destructive nuclear weapons from the first opening of hostilities until the bitter end, will invite war. The aggressor, taking into account hesitation and slow reaction in relation to the use of nuclear weapons in the counteraction, will more easily accept the calculated risk of starting war and especially nuclear aggression!

I know that, doubtless with the best intentions, many people with high ideals and an enormous love of humanity are campaining energetically for the banning of nuclear arms. As to the Communist leaders, we know from their behaviour that they do not have the same love of humanity and that consequently banning of nuclear weapons in N.A.T.O. hands would unquestionably bring the Western world closer to a new war. There are too many examples in recent times which prove that we cannot trust the Communists. They started in 1961 with a new and extensive number of nuclear tests, although there was a common agreement to stop the testing of nuclear weapons! The Communists have world domination in their program and their subversive actions all over the world prove that they have a very peculiar idea of peace. "World peace" has for the Communists the same meaning as "a world ruled by Communism". Everybody who does not accept Communist world domination is therefore against peace and will be accused by them as bellicose.

It is not the place here to give examples of Communist aggression. We all know how the Western Union and afterwards N.A.T.O., by integration and building up of military strength, has up till now avoided another world war.

A widespread conviction has developed that the tremendous destructive power of nuclear weapons—with which scientific progress has armed mankind—has made a Third World War increasingly improbable. The losses would be too high! Let us not forget that the Thirty Years' War in the seventeenth century cost the life of a third of the whole population of Germany! The behaviour of the Soviets in the East European countries, the concentration camps, etc. are facts which do not give us much confidence in them. The fact that our hope of escaping war is founded on the disastrous and destructive nature of a nuclear conflict, gives the aggressive nation the idea that its chance has come to destroy the other while it faces itself the minimum amount of retaliation it can ever hope to encounter. Do we really know ourselves what kind of arms arrangements would, and what kind would not increase the security of the free world against the danger of aggression and war? There are all kinds of reduction in armament, such as "balanced reduction", "phased reduction" or "proportionate reduction" of armaments, but the reduction of nuclear destructive power will always be the main problem. Probably there are people to-day who think, or assume without any logical and realistic thinking, that a a new great war is a contingency so remote that nobody needs to worry about it, while moreover the United Nations with their greater strength and psychological influence (as a world forum) should certainly be able to stop the next war. Recent experience has shown, however, that the United Nations lack the really objective and united power, but also the right appreciation for international law and justice, to be regarded as the trustworthy instrument to outlaw small and great conflicts. Nobody can deny that the two big world powers—the U.S.A. and the U.S.S.R.—are today deciding whether a local conflict (in Korea, or elsewhere) will grow into a larger conflict or not.

As long as there exists a balance of military power between East and West, it is quite obvious that war does not pay and peace will be safeguarded.

One may not have too much confidence in the working of a "balance of military power", "balance of terror" or "concept of stability", but as long as Communism has world domination as its principal political aim, we have no other trustworthy choice to safeguard world peace. Schelling gives us a description of what he thinks is the value of "stable". The "balance of deterrence" will be "stable" when political events, internal or external to the countries involved, technological changes, accidents, false alarms, misunderstandings, crises, limited wars, or changes in the intelligence available to both sides, are unlikely to disturb the incentives sufficiently to make mutual deterrence fail.[5]

For the time being this labile form of "stability" or "balance of deterrence" is the best we can obtain to reduce the risk of a Third World War. By now the opposing powers must have realized the disparity between costs and returns of a nuclear world conflict. In other words the indisputable fact that both—victor and vanquished—will emerge in a state of utter devastation, will have an appeasing influence. From a purely military point of view and with a realistic look at the present world situation we have therefore to maintain a "balance of deterrence" in order to safeguard peace. Just in line with the ideas explained here, President Kennedy said in his Inaugural Address: "The purpose in building our military strength is to avoid the necessity for its use!" All N.A.T.O. countries, too, are doing their best to strengthen N.A.T.O. in order to build up a force which really is an effective "balance of deterrence". Deterrence is a typical strategic concept and is concerned with influencing the choices that the aggressive party will make, and doing it by influencing his expectations of how we

5. T. C. Schelling and M. H. Halperin, Strategy and Arms Control, New York, 1961, p. 50.

12

will behave and use our ultimate weapons. It involves making the Communists believe the fact that N.A.T.O. behaviour will be determined by Soviet behaviour.

There are people in the free world and also in N.A.T.O. countries who think that, because no one wants a war, they—i.e. the statesmen and politicians—must see to it that we shall not have one. None of these statesmen in the N.A.T.O. countries has ever propagated aggression or war as a means of solving the present world problems. This cannot be said of the politicians from behind the Iron Curtain. During his state visit to Austria not so long ago, Khrushchev made a speech that leaves no doubt about the political aim of the Communists. He said for instance: "We are only alive a short while, and I would like to see the Red flag flying over the whole world during my lifetime. It would mean that Communism has been recognized everywhere as the best and noblest way of life and everything would be perfect".[6]

The political and military guarantee embodied in N.A.T.O. is the very condition of our freedom. Our existence in a free world, an example of social and scientific advancement, prosperity and a firm action to improve the life and economic development in backward countries of the free world, are essentially dependent on the maintenance of that guarantee!

The future of the world is decided by the two big blocs—N.A.T.O. and the Communists—and no other country, combination of states or organization will be able to influence the situation in the near future as they lack sufficient military power. We are living in a bi-polarized world! N.A.T.O. and the Soviet bloc possess sufficient quantities of atomic weapons to wipe each other out, even in the event of a Soviet surprise attack. The leaders in Moscow are just as well aware as we are that total war equals suicide. Suicide is the last thing an aggressive nation looking for world domination would like. There is no other outcome in the event of a total nuclear war than mutual obliteration. The Soviets may surrender to the temptation of taking into account the repugnance of N.A.T.O. to the idea of unleashing an atomic war, and therefore I think we would be taking a very high risk if N.A.T.O. were to give the Soviets the slightest hope that there is any chance that Soviet aggression will not be met immediately by an unlimited nuclear counterblow.

On the N.A.T.O. side there exists for the time being a "nuclear plenty", but concerning conventional forces N.A.T.O. is far behind in strength compared with the Soviets. Without giving up a large part of our prosperity and without a radical reduction in our aid to the

6. N.A.T.O. Letter, August 1960, p. 16.

underdeveloped countries, we shall be unable to reach a "conventional forces plenty" to safeguard peace. Therefore the Soviets are eager to ban nuclear weapons in order to obtain military superiority. Why should N.A.T.O. give up this tool of "nuclear plenty" or not use the effect of a "nuclear balance of terror" as long as this force is able to forestall Soviet aggression? Would it not be stupid to throw away our means of a real "deterrent" just to please the Soviets, giving them a chance to achieve their political aim of world domination without risking complete destruction. N.A.T.O. is only able to safeguard peace by maintaining its superiority in military power through scientific progress, perfection of our weapon systems, integration, standardization and so on. That is the way to maintain the "balance of terror". The nuclear weapons still constitute the very basis of our deterrent and it is a question of to be or not to be in keeping N.A.T.O. ahead in the development of new and still more effective weapon systems, in order to force the Soviets to relinquish any thought of aggression.

Today in order to maintain the "balance of terror" we have to pay full attention as well to what is called by M. N. Golovine "aerospace power". He writes: "Very gradually the world status of nation unarmed in orbit and space will deteriorate and their influence in world affairs diminish accordingly. An orbital conflict between two major Powers, without the possibility of any other nation influencing its outcome, will demonstrate the unfortunate but evident futility of "words without weapons" and create a growing sense of insecurity among the population of the globe".[7] I will not review all the possibilities of spacecraft for military use but it is to be hoped that the United States of America will succeed in closing the "Aerospace Gap" as soon as possible. The manned space vehicles of the Soviets are a real threat to the West. For that reason not only the U.S.A., but also the European N.A.T.O. countries must concentrate all their scientific knowledge and scientists on the development of space vehicles. Western Europe has a considerable cadre of technicians and scientists, able to develop its own space vehicles. The electronic and aeronautic industry of Europe must not lag behind in this new field of astronautics. The scientific potential of Europe may also be of high value to the U.S.A. to close as soon as possible the "Aerospace Gap". The Soviet threat in space must not be underestimated! We cannot risk lagging behind in this new field of military armament!

Looking at the present political situation in our bi-polarized world and at the purely military aspects of that situation, we cannot overlook—in connexion with the problems of the underdeveloped nations

7. M. N. Golovine, Conflict in Space, London, 1962, p. 115.

of the free world—the fact that a lot of these countries are—because of their geographic location—very important for N.A.T.O. In the theory of the balance of deterrence N.A.T.O. has to pay all its attention to the existing and very serious danger that especially Western Europe can be cut off from certain parts of the world which deliver strategic raw materials or are essential markets for our peace as well as war economy. This is not the place to discuss the military strategic importance of the countries of the free world situated south of the Soviet territory. All I want to say is that there is no military force in the Middle East or in South Asia able to hold a Soviet aggression with the intention of occupying the Middle East and subsequently the northern part of Africa. Our N.A.T.O. partner Turkey, not being so advanced in its economic development as most of the other N.A.T.O. countries, must be considered of the highest strategic value. It is therefore of the greatest importance—and even more important than our aid to the backward nations—to help Turkey to become a very strong nation, both from a military and an economic viewpoint, safeguarding the south-eastern flank of N.A.T.O. Greece, although more advanced than Turkey, also needs our full interest. All we want is to maintain the status quo in that part of the world. For the time being there does not exist either in the Middle East or in the northern part of Africa a military force able to resist a Soviet attack. For that reason it is of the greatest importance to N.A.T.O. that the countries in those areas (Asia, Middle East and the whole northern part of Africa) should be developing rapidly and that the existing military gap should be filled up by nations with well-founded independent governments, having not only a sound economic and social system but also an adequate defence.

Aid given to those countries will be just as important, from a purely military point of view, as aid given to other underdeveloped countries for economic reasons.

The reader may be wondering why I started this study about the relations between N.A.T.O. and the developing countries with a purely strategic survey, but one has to realize that there will be neither a N.A.T.O. nor a free world once the balance of military power is lost. It is true that we shall not solve the controversy between East and West with this "balance of terror", but we are forcing the Soviets and their satellites to use other methods as long as they intend to continue their struggle for world domination. Although it is no solution of the world problems, it is useful to know that without underestimating these problems we may be able to solve them without force of arms.

I really am not a prophet and my ideas cannot be more than an analysis and a prognosis of the world situation in which nuclear weapons play the most important role, and in the near future also space vehicles. Although my conclusion is hypothetical, it is my firm belief that no global war will occur as long as a reciprocal threat of an all-out nuclear war exists and the parties concerned are not left in doubt about the instantaneous use of nuclear weapons by the N. A. T. O. forces. The potential opponents will not gamble on this matter but will determine their actions after a very realistic assessment of the risks involved. Disparity between returns and costs of a nuclear conflict will—and there can be no doubt about this—leave the aggressor and the attacked in a state of utter devastation! It sounds perhaps paradoxical but the development and increase of nuclear weapons is the best and irreplaceable instrument for safeguarding peace. . . but also will only be of the highest value if there is no doubt about their use to counter aggression without any delay!

We are all aware of the existence of the "Iron Curtain" and we look at it as the barrier between East and West. However, this picture is misleading. We are wrong when we think that this wall has to be seen as a crystallization of the split between East and West.

Communism is infiltrating in all parts of the world and the leaders of the U.S.S.R. are doing their very best to set up a large number of new "iron curtains" in the free world with the sole purpose of weakening the position of the N.A.T.O. bloc and of making peaceful co-operation impossible between nations in a free world.

As long as the "balance of deterrence" makes it impossible for the Communists to dominate the world, they must use other methods in order to attain their political aim, corresponding with the doctrine of Lenin: "The object of the party is to exploit all and any conflicting interests among the surrounding capitalist groups and governments with a view to disintegrating capitalism".

The Soviet Union—becoming convinced that the triumph of Communism achieved by the use of arms has to be given up—is now obliged to alter fundamentally its tactics to reach the old Leninist objective. We were told by Khrushchev in 1957, during an interview for the Columbia Broadcasting system in the U. S. A. what tactics will be used. He said: "We think that capitalism should be destroyed not by means of war and military conflicts but through an ideological and economic struggle. During a speech at Novosibirsk Khrushchev gave an even more accurate explanation of the tactics Communism will use. So quote: "Peaceful coexistence must be properly understood. It represents a continuation of the struggle between two social systems, but a

16

struggle carried on by peaceful means, without war and without interference in the internal affairs of other countries. For us it is an economic, political and ideological struggle, not a trial of military strength". I think it is useful to cite more statements by Mr. Khrushchev and his Soviet colleagues to know exactly where we stand and what we have to expect. In 1958, Khrushchev said that the Seven Year Plan would be "a decisive step towards implementing the basic economic task of the U.S.S.R.—to catch up with and overtake in the historically shortest period of time the most highly developed capitalist countries in per capita output of goods".

One of the leading papers of the Soviet Communist Party, "Kommunist", recalled that "the development of socialism leads to the formation of a single world socialist economy . . . (which) will only take place with the victory of Communism on a world scale". Thus all the Russian economic activities are always subordinated to the destruction of the capitalist system and to the political needs of the U.S.S.R.

"Peaceful coexistence" is one of the favourite slogans of the Communist leaders since the nuclear threat has made war an unworkable tool. Coexistence in the Communist thinking is not defensive but aggressive; it is not a protection against war but a substitute for it. The best way to define what "peaceful coexistence" really means is: the form in which today the big struggle for world domination can be fought under the balance of atomic terror. The Communists like to achieve their aims without risking war, dismantling the Western economic position not by force but in a series of relatively painless and well-camouflaged small operations, slicing away piecemeal one Western position—essential for the Western economy and prosperity—after another.

The Communist leaders do not hide their objectives and they tell us that they are doing their level best to undermine our economic system in the broadest sense and with all means.

Therefore our principal N.A.T.O. objective must now be—and is likely to remain—the preservation of a strong, free and viable Western world. This implies the necessity to safeguard all sources of vital importance to the strategic and economic existence of N.A.T.O.

When we are speaking here of "peace", we have to consider that we in the free world have an absolutely different idea of the meaning of "peace" from the Communists. We are talking of peace when the fighting is over and we do everything to return to good relations with the former enemies. The Communists, however, continue their way by every means short of the actual use of military weapons. To them world domination and revolution is preordained by history!

17

Taking this into account, we will not be surprised to know that "peaceful coexistence" has for the Communists no other meaning than an economic, political and ideological struggle, but without a trial of military strength.

Consequently N.A.T.O. and all the countries belonging to this organization have to be constantly alert and must keep a close watch on all the Communist activities and manifestations of that "modern offensive". We must look on this type of war as the "real war", though with other means than we should historically identify as weapons!

The decisive struggle for supremacy today will not be fought with spacecraft, guided weapons, etc., but will be fought in the economic and psychological field, not forgetting technological and scientific activities either.

Having safeguarded our defence with the most modern weapon systems, such as nuclear weapons, guided missiles, electronic counter-measures, etc., and also safeguarded our strategic positions from where a counter-attack after Soviet aggression can effectively be launched—this being altogether the only way to extort peace from the U.S.S.R. to the benefit of mankind all over the world—we still have to compete with the Communists in the economic field. Taking into account the interdependence of nations in relation to their economic existence and growth, N.A.T.O. must pay full attention to the underdeveloped countries.

N.A.T.O. has a very great role to play. N.A.T.O. is the anchor of defence of the free world but also the only guarantee of the liberty and prosperity of our own countries. With our alliance we must set up a barrier against the expansion of Communism and guarantee the development of the backward countries in a political, economic and cultural sense as well as in an atmosphere of freedom, reciprocal understanding and co-operation. We must bear in mind that the mere existence of N.A.T.O. is not enough in itself—an enormous effort of will-power and determination will be required in order to obtain success. Weakness, ethical principles, unrealistic self-sacrifice and so on will not safeguard a free world but will on the contrary invite suppression and slavery. For that reason we must take a firm stand today with a very realistic look at the political situation and without prejudicing people against ourselves. The human, political, and social revolution and evolution in many parts of the free world outside the N.A.T.O. area is without any doubt the great challenge of our day. It is of the greatest importance for the developing new nations, as well as for the Western world, that this revolution should take place in an atmosphere of freedom and without any threat of political

18

moves. We must also ensure that these new nations do not succumb to Communist domination, by unravelling the carefully camouflaged propaganda and misleading promises of the Communists.

It may not be wrong to express my opinion that we are living today in a pre-war period with an increasing threat of military force, resulting from the accelerating arms race. On the other hand we are in a much better situation compared with the pre-war period leading us to the First and the Second World War, because the price in destruction that the new weapon systems represent on both sides may do what paper pacts could never do, namely rule out major war as an ultimate instrument of policy.

The disappearance of alternatives, the narrowing of choice, the progressive loss of domination by governments as a result of the nuclear weapons, are forcing the responsible political leaders to use other methods to reach their principal political aim.

In the past—even in the near past—we were able to discern the difference between war and peace, because it was quite as distinct as the difference between black and white. Nowadays our modern society is very complicated and consequently very vulnerable to hostile psychological and economic actions. However harmless they may look at first sight, these actions are just as dangerous as any military aggression and will be of ever-increasing importance in undermining our existence.

When we speak of peace in the military sense, it does not mean that there is no fighting at all. What we today call "cold war" is nothing else but a war going on with other means than military forces. It is a form of warfare and of aggression by which an aggressive nation or alliance tries to achieve its political end without the use of military weapons. For the Communists this end is world domination. Political, psychological and economic means are the weapons used in the cold war. When we are dealing in this study with the defence of N.A.T.O. and in connexion with the importance of the backward nations in the free world, we will limit ourselves to the economic aspects, although sometimes we will be unable to by-pass political and psychological aspects.

N.A.T.O. is to a high degree dependent upon a variety of economic factors, which are variously interpreted and defined. Most writers who stress the importance of economic factors are referring to the economic strength of the nations, as distinct from their military forces or in relation to economic war preparation and industrial mobilization in time of war. In my opinion any attack on our peace economy, any disturbance of the economic system in the free world and especially in the highly industrialized Western society, may result in more or less serious disaster.

There is at present an enormous and merciless economic battle going on and the Communists are making an all-out effort to undermine the position of the N.A.T.O. countries and to put a wedge between N.A.T.O. and the rest of the free world. Neither any nation nor any alliance is able to survive without a regular flow of certain raw materials, a world-wide trading system or reciprocal aid, as long as full employment, prosperity for all, economic growth and above all independence and freedom are the main aim. The economic system of our present world is so complicated that for our existence in time of peace or war, we are dependent upon each other. That means that the developing and underdeveloped countries, wherever they may be geographically located, are drawn into the controversy between East and West, whether they like it or not.

We realize that what is economically desirable is not always politically desirable, if not politically possible. Too often the economic threat of the Soviets is not only overlooked by the politicians, but even by the economists.

The political aim of N.A.T.O. is not and has never been world domination. All we want is co-operation in freedom. Nobody can deny that a nation gains by the prosperity of other nations and not by their poverty. The world's political organization has not kept pace with its economic organization and still less with the mutual economic dependence. Raw materials, markets, loans, private investments, trade routes, prices, technical assistance, etc. are things in which the various peoples of the world have a joint as well as a seperate interest.

The nations of the Atlantic Alliance as well as the newly independent—more or less underdeveloped—countries have one common interest, prosperity and freedom for all.

CHAPTER II

THE ECONOMIC VULNERABILITY OF N.A.T.O.

The speech which Khrushchev made at the Twenty-Second Party Congress set forth an ambitious plan for an accelerating economic growth and industrial development during the next twenty years. This Soviet plan envisages the making of the U.S.S.R. into a huge material and technical base. The Kremlin has in mind not only to catch up with the U.S.A. in industrial output but even to overtake the N.A.T.O. countries as a whole. Although the Communist leaders pretend that this extended program is necessary to crush any aggressor who dares to raise his hand against the U.S.S.R., their actual target is to build up a force able to overthrow N.A.T.O.

Let nobody assume that the Soviets or the Chinese Communists have given up their aim of world domination, although there has been, thank goodness, no military aggression up till now.

The Communists have never relied solely on military power to achieve their ends. We know how they have used propaganda and subversion. For a couple of years now they have been using economic penetration as a new weapon, and the economic growth of the U.S.S.R. has given them a chance to put more emphasis on economic penetration and other economic measures. Since 1954 the Communists have started to use economic programmes to obtain greater influence in the underdeveloped countries.

The Soviet politico-economic action is based on the Leninist doctrine "The object of the party is to exploit all and any conflicting interest among the surrounding capitalist groups and governments with a view to disintegrating capitalism" and, as we mentioned before Khrushchev also threatened the West with an economic contest.

We do not have any objection against the Soviet aim to catch up with N.A.T.O. in per capita output of goods. If the aim of the Soviet economic growth is to bring prosperity to the Russians and also to the populations of the underdeveloped countries—without loss of freedom—we can only appreciate the Communists' intentions. We do not envy the Russians or other people getting more and better consumer goods, better housing and a higher standard of living. However, if the aim of the Soviet leaders is to use the increased economic power to reinforce the Communist military power in order to dominate

21

the world, establishing that domination by military aggression, there is a serious cause for alarm. As the Soviet leaders have repeated time and time again that their basic long-term aims remain unchanged—namely to destroy the institutions of the N.A.T.O. countries and to undermine the powers and ideas which support them, using all their resources, military, economic and subversive, to secure this aim—we cannot take any risk. For the present the Soviets give first priority to the economic weapon only to undermine N.A.T.O., as well as getting their hands free to overrule in the next phase the backward nations, who have practically no defence at their disposal nor the means to build up an adequate military force to defend themselves. The more or less underdeveloped nations—most of them newly independent, and more of them will be so in the near future—are struggling for economic progress and national identification. The Communists are seeking to promote their political objectives, aiming at a reduction of the influence of the N.A.T.O. countries, but also at a disruption of the defensive alliances of the free world and an increase of their own power and prestige, by aid and technical assistance to under-developed nations and also increased trade.

The great difference between the West and the Communists in their relations with the underdeveloped countries is that, while we desire to see them politically and economically independent, the Communists want to see them dependent if not submissive in these two fields.

Political leaders too often underestimate the Soviet economic threat. The economic weapon is a very dangerous weapon and especially in our present highly industrialized Western world. The economic threat is more difficult to discover than the military, but may be even far more mortal. Nuclear weapons have an immense destructive power, but the economic weapon can be just as devastating, because it is able to disorganize completely our whole Western economic system.

One may ask if we really are so vulnerable. A Western economy is not a set of isolated pieces of technology, but a technical and cultural complex. It is based upon the ready availability of materials, compo-nents, tools and technological knowledge. It depends on a compli-cated network of communication and transportation facilities, as well as on auxiliary enterprises providing financial, managerial and tech-nical facilities and a complex system of business practices. The level of our economic development is manifested in the amount of accumu-lated per capita social wealth, labour productivity, the level of technical equipment and finally in the norms of output and consumption per head of population. For that reason the economic structure of the Western nations is very vulnerable. The rapid economic growth in the recent past increased the problems we have to face and accordingly increased the vulnerability of our present society. The nations of the Atlantic Alliance are as a result of the rapid technological progress highly industrialized. Mechanization and the use of more efficient methods lessened the number of people that could be engaged in agriculture, forcing them to find a job in industry or elsewhere. The steady growth of the population in the Western world made it necessary to stimulate industrialization and trade in order to create jobs and a reasonable way of living for all. The regularly growing economy in the last decade extended modern technology over the whole front of our economic activity. The make-up of the Western economy changed unceasingly as techniques improved, new industries accelerated and obsolete industries failed and disappeared. The economies of the Western nations found their place in the international economy. The economies, concentrated in the beginning of the industrial period around a relatively narrow complex of industry and technological progress, have extended their range into more perfected and technologically more complex processes. So a stage was reached in which the economies demonstrated that they had the technological and entrepreneurial skills to produce those goods giving the highest profits. The import of raw materials from elsewhere, and also the development and growth of the means of transportation and communication, facilitated the economic growth into maturity.

A nation's economic life calls for a vast and delicate balancing of multitudinous resources against continually changing needs and demands.

The changing pattern of the materials we use has thrown the minerals and a number of agricultural products into sharp focus. Year after year the industries of the Western nations needed and used more and more raw and other materials to manufacture the manifold products that the continuously expanding economies demand.

There is no doubt that the momentum of the pre-war economy of the United States of America and the post-war economy of the West European countries was reflected substantially by a widespread boom in consumer goods and services. The result was the acceptance and absorption of the age of high mass consumption.

Mass production resulted in a still further increased demand for raw materials as well as in a dynamic development of world trade, while it also substantially increased prosperity in terms of consumption per head and more social security.

When we look at the high percentage of the population of the Western nations engaged in the production of capital and consumer goods, transportation, public utilities, administration and trade, we realize how important it is that our present economic system should not be disrupted. Specialization, cost of labour, climatic conditions, availability of raw materials, made interchanging of goods and services between the advanced countries possible. However, there are two factors we must not overlook and certainly not underestimate: the problem of the raw materials and the need for markets where we can sell our products.

Within N.A.T.O. and still more within the Western world we have at our disposal in the required quantities and qualities most of the raw materials we need for our economic activities. However, there are some raw materials and agricultural products we have to obtain partly or entirely from the underdeveloped nations. Some of these raw materials are essential for our economies and in those cases we are dependent on their import from nations of the free world outside the Atlantic Alliance. In a free world there cannot be the slightest objection against this dependency, as long as they are available on the world market, or can be obtained by bilateral agreements.

As soon as these essential raw materials we need from outside the Western world are no longer available to us, we may be in a sorry plight. It will not always be possible to replace them by substitutes and if we are able to use substitutes, it may take research a long time before these materials are produced in the required quantities and then often at much higher cost. The past has shown how the Suez affair and the resulting decrease of the oil flow to Western Europe led to a rationing of gasoline in a number of European countries, in order not to disturb too seriously the various economic systems. Although there was enough oil available in the free world, the blockade of the Suez Canal already resulted in an interruption of some industrial activities. This event showed the strategic importance of a nation controlling any part of the communication lines between the sources of raw materials and the West, giving us another reason why N.A.T.O. is obliged to maintain good relationships with underdeveloped countries and give them aid or assistance in any form. Once we are lacking certain raw materials, other industries—not using these in their production processes—will also be influenced. Lack of essential raw materials in peacetime as a result of certain political events may lead to unemployment, will affect our prosperity and also more or less disorganize our economic system. For that reason we must take full interest in the underdeveloped nations possessing those raw materials we are in urgent need of. Moreover there is the possibility that the Communists may try, by means of trade agreements with certain underdeveloped countries, to lay their hands on raw materials essential for the West, not needed by them but in order to influence our economy. So it will be clear that it is a must for N.A.T.O. to pay full attention to the problems

24

of the backward nations, in order to safeguard our own peace economy.

When the Korean conflict started we saw an enormous increase in the demand for raw materials, resulting in a sharp rise in prices. These higher prices had a direct influence upon the balances of payments of the more or less highly industrialized Western nations. It is not the place here to go into all the economic consequences of a rise in the price of raw materials and the resulting influences of that rise on the export possibilities.

In addition to the human resources, there are the material resources—the agricultural, energy and mineral resources—without which a society cannot exist. All human activity will be dominated by the availability of raw materials. The increase in the world's population during the next few decades will create an increasing need for the metallic and non-metallic raw materials of mineral origin, but likewise for agricultural products. This applies, first of all, to the highly industrialized countries whose manufacturing output represents a considerable, if not an overwhelming, part of their national product. We all know that at present no nation is self-sufficient in the field of raw materials. Since 1900 the growth of the world's industrial machine has been so dynamic that in every advanced nation large quantities of raw materials are required. Technological progress, especially in the making of metals for special purposes, has created a need for certain raw materials which are found only in isolated pockets scattered over the surface of our planet. Few problems are likely to be more important in the near future than those of the nations that are now characterized as underdeveloped; that importance has grown as a result of the raw materials those countries have at their disposal.

Talking about raw materials, we also have to pay attention to the growing need for agricultural products and especially for foodstuffs. The world's population has been increasing rapidly, exerting intensive pressure on the productive capacity of the available arable land. This holds good especially for the advanced societies but also for a lot of underdeveloped countries.

Table I shows the development of the population of the world and of various continents and proves the truth of this proposition.

In some countries enough arable land may be available to produce the required food for the increased population, but in others, especially in a number of European countries, food will have to be imported in larger quantities. Although mechanization of agriculture and the use of various kinds of fertilizers has increased the output of food and agricultural products for the industry, that will very often not be sufficient to meet our requirements.

The food problem in North America, where a huge quantity of

Table I

POPULATION GROWTH OF THE WORLD AND VARIOUS CONTINENTS IN PERIOD 0-2000
(millions of people)

Year	World	Africa	North America	Latin America	Asia	Europe
0	300	50	—	—	200	50
1650	500	100	1	10	300	100
1800	900	100	6	20	600	200
1850	1,100	100	26	33	700	274
1900	1,600	130	81	63	900	423
1920	1,810	140	117	91	966	487
1930	2,013	155	135	109	1,072	532
1940	2,246	172	146	131	1,212	573
1950	2,494	198	168	163	1,376	576
1955	2,691	223	183	183	1,481	606
1960	2,950	237	199	204	1,656	642
2000 *	6,267	517	312	592	3,870	947

* U.N. calculations, average hypothesis in "De Malthus à Mao-Tsé Toung, Alfred Sauvy," p. 27.
Source: "Bevolkingsexplosies", W. Brand, p. 8.

arable land is still available, need not be taken too seriously; on the contrary in Western Europe this problem demands increased attention.

Although table II does not show such an explosive growth of population in the European N.A.T.O. countries as in other regions of the world, we have to reckon with a relative decrease of agricultural production.

The more we industrialize Western Europe, the more arable land has to be used for the new industrial plants, which will force us to import more agricultural products from elsewhere. This will result in an increased dependence for these products on the underdeveloped countries of Asia, Africa and Latin America, although North America may partly help us out of the problem. In addition there are also a number of tropical agricultural products that have to be imported from underdeveloped countries.

Practically no nation, and especially not the European industrialized countries, is independent in regard to raw materials. In this respect the United States and Canada are much more self-sufficient, although a small number of essential raw materials have still to be obtained from elsewhere. The increase of the population of the N.A.T.O. countries will create a growing need for metallic and non-metallic raw materials of mineral origin. Furthermore the per capita consumption

26

Table II

POPULATION OF EUROPEAN N.A.T.O. COUNTRIES
IN DIFFERENT YEARS
(thousands of people)

Country	1940	1950	1955	1960
Belgium	8,301	8,639	8,868	9,153
Denmark	3,832	4,271	4,439	4,581
France	39,800	41,736	43,279	45,542
(Western) Germany	—	47,847	50,176	53,373
Greece	7,319	7,566	7,966	8,327
Iceland	121	143	158	176
Italy	43,840	46,603	48,064	49,361
Luxemburg	296	297	309	314
Netherlands	8,879	10,114	10,751	11,480
Norway	2,973	3,265	3,429	3,586
Portugal	7,696	8,405	8,765	8,921
Turkey	17,821	20,947	24,065	27,561
United Kingdom	48,226	50,616	51,221	52,539
Total:	189,104	250,449	261,490	274,914

Source: Demographic Yearbook 1960 U.N.

of these raw materials is likely to increase with the rise of prosperity. The more the manufacturing output represents a substantial part of the national product, the more the necessity of import of raw materials will be a question of serious concern, because the consumption of mineral raw materials depends largely on the size of the manufacturing output. The continuous changes in methods of production as a result of technological progress and research have also led to changes in the required assortment of raw materials. Iron and steel are likely to retain their predominant position in the manufacturing industry, but today ferro-alloying minerals such as cobalt, manganese, vanadium, nickel, chromite and titanium are necessary to give steel the special qualities demanded by modern machinery. The non-ferrous metals such as aluminium, lead, magnesium and copper are also indispensable in modern production. The more advanced the products we are making, such as supersonic aircraft or spacecraft, the more serious is the problem of raw materials. On the other hand plastics and other artificial materials have replaced a number of raw materials we always used. We have also replaced a number of natural products by synthetic materials. Synthetic rubber has partly replaced natural caoutchouc. I suppose that nobody is able to say beforehand that he will continue to be independent for raw materials of other nations, although he may be self-sufficient to a high degree for the present. The introduction of synthetic materials may be a very serious handicap for those underdeveloped countries which export raw materials, and particularly when they are to a large extent dependent on that export for their economic growth and balance of payments. However, the progress of science has also created a demand for products that used to be of little value in the past. Oranges have always been used as fruit and the orange-juice was tinned. The profit was not very high. Today the orange-juice is no longer the most important substance of an orange, for margarine and a colouring matter for rayon are also extracted from the pips; the peel produces a dye-stuff and carotine. From the latter vitamin A is obtained. The white pulp gives pectine, a preservative, and further these oranges produce vitamin B, ethyl alcohol and a few other products.

This example proves that the agricultural products of underdeveloped countries may prove to be of much higher value when chemical research results in new discoveries. Nobody could foresee that an orange farm would ever develop into a chemical factory! The production and consumption of energy are indices that assist in the determination of a nation's economic potential. Generally speaking oil, coal and water-power are the most important elements for producing energy, but also natural gas will soon be used in large quantities as a source of energy. Oil is the second great energy source available to advanced nations, but there are good reasons to anticipate that natural gas and atomic energy will replace coal to a large extent. Hydroelectric power will play a still further diminishing role in Western Europe, although it is a not too expensive source of energy.

Natural gas is found both in N.A.T.O. countries and in the underdeveloped countries, but the underdeveloped world supplies the greater part of uranium, our latest source of energy.

Nature has distributed raw materials all over the world and there is no link between political, cultural and economic importance and the possession of raw materials in the national soil.

Climatic reasons also have restricted the output of certain agricultural products to certain regions. Therefore our conclusion must be that N.A.T.O. countries are for some or other raw material, foodstuff or other agricultural product dependent on one or more underdeveloped countries.

As soon as the flow of raw materials to N.A.T.O. countries and especially to highly industrialized Western Europe is interrupted, we will find ourselves in trouble. Table III shows the size and density of the population per sq km in Western Europe and a study of this table in connexion with the figures of the growth of population (table I and II)—particularly in regard to Europe—leads to the conclusion that we shall never be able to maintain or to expand our manufac-

28

Table III

POPULATION SIZE AND DENSITY PER sq. km
OF EUROPEAN N.A.T.O. COUNTRIES
(with a population above 9 million)

1960	people	density per sq. km
(Western) Germany	53,4	213
UK	52,5	214
Italy	49,4	163
France	45,5	82
Turkey	26,9	31 in Asia 90 in Europe
Netherlands	11,5	350
Belgium & Luxemburg	9,5	298

Source: Demographic Yearbook 1960 U.N.

turing capacity and our economy in the required measure, as soon as we are getting short of essential raw materials. Unemployment, loss of prosperity and disorganization of our economic system will be the result.

The sources of raw materials, partly located in the underdeveloped countries, are very important pillars of our peace economy. As we mentioned before, the European N.A.T.O. countries are in this respect very vulnerable and to a much higher degree than the U.S.A. or Canada. Table IV shows the raw materials for which the various N.A.T.O. countries are dependent on imports and also shows the dependence for them on various underdeveloped nations. What we have written about the importance of raw materials for our peace economy holds good still more with regard to our war economy.

The hunger for raw materials in time of war, as a result of the wastage of weapons and equipment, is frightening. Governments are well aware of that and by stockpiling they are trying to decrease the vulnerability in regard to essential raw materials. Stockpiling is a very expensive business and therefore it may be preferable to set limits to stockpiling only for the first critical period of the war and to depend for the rest on the sources of raw materials in the underdeveloped countries. The latter will only be possible if we are sure that the flow of essential raw materials in time of political tension or war will not be cut off or blockaded by strategically well-located hostile nations.

I will not review all the problems concerning stockpiling, as it is enough to have demonstrated the dependence of N.A.T.O. on backward nations for our war economy and the necessity for that reason to be interested in the economic drive to maturity of these underdeveloped

TOTAL IMPORTS OF RAW MATERI*

Total imports for NATO-countries 1960	1 Rice		2 Maize		3 Sugar	
Countries of origin	Quantity	Value	Quantity	Value	Quantity	Va*
AFRICA						
Algeria	500	100				
Egypt	26.900	2500			71.500	18*
Ethiopia + Eritrea						
Rep. of the Middle Congo						
Ghana						
Guinea						
Cameroons						
Liberia						
Libya						
Morocco	3900	1000	67.100	4000		
Rhodesia			44.200	2900		
Portuguese Africa			66.400	3800	150.300	15.2
Sudan						
Tunesia						
Togoland						
Malagasy Rep.	16.600	4600			8500	14*
Congo + Ruanda Urundi					8800	16*
Nigeria						
Total	47.900	8200	177.700	10.700	239.100	20.0*
ASIA						
Afghanistan						
Burma	56.400	3800				
Cambodia	54.000	4200				
China-Taiwan						
India					5300	1*
Ceylon						
Iraq						
Iran						
Indonesia					69.700	17*
Israël						
Japan						
Jordan						
Laos						
Malaya Fed.						
Pakistan						
Syria						
Thailand	38.000	5000				
South-Vietnam	15.200	1400				
Saudi-Arabia						
Singapore						
Libanon						
Philippines						
Total	163.600	14.400			75.000	18*

* Excl. the U.S.

Note: Quantity in tons; for iron ore and petroleum in thousands tons; value in thous* of US $ c.i.f.

Source: Calculated from OEEC Statistical Bulletins: 'Foreign Trade, series C, Trade Commodities, Vol. II: imports' (1960).

	4		5		6		7	
	Oil seeds + oil nuts		Wool and other animal hair		Cotton		Jute	
	Quantity	Value	Quantity	Value	Quantity	Value	Quantity	Value
	12.100	300	700	700	500	300		
	2.800	700			84.800	74.900		
E	16.500	3000			200	200		
	13.500	2400			26.800	16.300		
	5700	1000						
	2100	300						
	15.700	2800			6800	4300		
	9100	1500						
	8100	2300	400	300				
	10.500	1700	2900	3000	1000	800		
	12.600	3000			1800	1200		
	91.700	14.000			52.400	31.600		
	136.400	17.800			65.700	57.600		
	800	100	200	200				
	23.600	3800			2900	1400		
R	6900	1600			700	400		
	20.700	3700			37.300	21.600		
	731.700	129.900			21.900	13.300		
	1120.500	189.900	4200	4200	302.800	223.900		
			300	300	800	600		
					7500	3700	400	100
	18.400	5400	10.100	11.500	22.800	4700	2900	600
			600*	600*	900	500		
			400*	10.800	26.900	16.500		
	48.000	10.000						
	3200	1100			200	100		
					2300	400		
	17.800	3300						
	3600	600	6900*	8900*	21.400	8500	447.000	117.900
	9000	800			46.700	26.100		
	2600	400					18.300	3100
	6800	1700						
	2000	300			400	200		
	442.400	93.400						
	553.800	117.000	18.300	32.100	129.900	61.300	468.600	121.700

TOTAL IMPORTS OF RAW MATERIA

Total imports for NATO-countries 1960	8		9		10	
	Crude rubber		Iron ore		Lead ore	
Countries of origin	Quantity	Value	Quantity	Value	Quantity	Valu
AFRICA						
Algeria			3700	41.000	10.100	1!
Egypt			100	1100		
Ethiopia + Eritrea						
Rep. of the Middle Congo	600	500			41.700	8:
Ghana	500	400				
Guinea			400	4300		
Cameroons	3100	2400				
Liberia	42.600	35.300	2300	32.000		
Libya						
Morocco			1600	21.800	106.800	12.*
Rhodesia						
Portuguese Africa			600	9300		
Sudan						
Tunesia			1000	12.100		
Togoland						
Malagasy Rep.						
Congo + Ruanda Urundi	30.400	23.300				
Nigeria	53.500	39.600				
Total	130.700	101.500	9700	121.600	158.600	22.
ASIA						
Afghanistan						
Burma	3800	3000				
Cambodia	18.400	12.700				
China-Taiwan	200	200				
India			200	2900		
Ceylon	37.900	31.900				
Iraq						
Iran						
Indonesia	176.700	129.700				
Israël					4900	2
Japan						
Jordan						
Laos						
Malaya Fed.	507.900	409.700	100	1400	600	4
Pakistan						
Syria						
Thailand	71.600	53.400				
South-Vietnam	65.300	52.000				
Saudi-Arabia						
Singapore	76.500	62.000				
Libanon						
Philippines						
Total	958.300	754.600	300	4300	5500	2!

* Excl. the U.S.

	11		12		13		14	
	Zinc ore		Manganese ore		Silver and Platinum ores		Copper (unwrought)	
	Quantity	Value	Quantity	Value	Quantity	Value	Quantity	Value
-E	71.700	5300	81.600	1800			600	500
ï			3200	200				
]			387.600	25.300				
A	87.400	5500	358.500	17.300			392.500*	268.400
			18.400	1400			2900*	1800
			34.300	1900				
•	6300	400						
R -R	101.100	4200	208.400	10.000			290.900	191.700
	266.500	15.400	1092.000	57.900			686.900	462.400
T	22.900	1500					400	100
	21.900	1100						
F								
V A								
	44.800	2600					400	100

TOTAL IMPORTS OF RAW MATERIA

Total imports for NATO-countries 1960	15		16		17	
	Nickel (unwrought)		Aluminium (unwrought)		Tin (unwrought)	
Countries of origin	Quantity	Value	Quantity	Value	Quantity	Valu
AFRICA						
Algeria						
Egypt						
Ethiopia + Eritrea						
Rep. of the Middle Congo						
Ghana						
Guinea						
Cameroons			38.000*	18.600		
Liberia						
Libya						
Morocco						
Rhodesia						
Portuguese Africa						
Sudan						
Tunesia						
Togoland						
Malagasy Rep.						
Congo + Ruanda Urundi					3900	86(
Nigeria						
Total			38.000	18.600	3900	86(
ASIA						
Afghanistan						
Burma						
Cambodia						
China-Taiwan						
India						
Ceylon						
Iraq						
Iran						
Indonesia					1400	33(
Israël						
Japan						
Jordan						
Laos						
Malaya Fed.					44.700	102.00
Pakistan						
Syria						
Thailand						
South-Vietnam						
Saudi-Arabia						
Singapore					1400	29(
Libanon						
Philippines						
Fr. Oceania	13.500	14.900				
Total	13.500	14.900			47.500	108.2(

† Excl. Canada.
* Excl. the U.S.

| | 18 | | 19 | | 20 | | 21 | |
| | Lead (unwrought) | | Zinc (unwrought) | | Petroleum (unwrought) | | Inorganic chemicals | |
	Quantity	Value	Quantity	Value	Quantity	Value	Quantity	Value
	1800	400			6900	149.900		
+E					600	8900		
h					800	15.700		
u								
	23.700†*	4400†*					1400	100
A	800†*	200†*	1300	300				
							1000	100
	15.600†*	3300†*			300	7300		
R								
+R			8400	6200				
					1000	18.700		
	41.900	8300	9700	6500	9600	200.500	2400	200
T							500	100
					33.000	617.300		
					20.600†	409.800		
					4000	55.500		
							4000	500
					200	4900	900†*	10.800
F								
					3100	69.400		
V					26.700†	465.500		
A					2200	42.300		
					89.800	1664.700	5400	11.400

TOTAL IMPORTS OF RAW MATERIA

Total imports for NATO-countries 1960	1		2		3	
	Rice		Maize		Sugar	
Countries of origin	Quantity	Value	Quantity	Value	Quantity	Value
CENTRAL AMERICA						
Guatemala						
Honduras						
Nicaragua						
Mexico			368.800	19.900	34.000	320
Dominican Rep.					409.500	32.20
Total			368.800	19.900	443.500	35.40
SOUTH AMERICA						
Argentinia	2000	100	2.436.200	142.200	9000	80
Bolivia						
Brazil			6100	400	171.300	13.80
Chile						
Colombia						
Ecuador					30.100	70
Br. Guiana						
Fr. Guiana						
Surinam + Ant.	14.200	2000			7100	50
Paraguay			9500	500	2200	20
Peru			800	100	68.300	550
Uruguay						
Venezuela						
French West Indies					192.000	32.00
Total	16.200	2100	2.452.600	143.200	480.000	53.50

* Excl. the U.S.

36

	4		5		6		7	
	Oil seeds + oil nuts		Wool and other animal hair		Cotton		Jute	
	Quantity	Value	Quantity	Value	Quantity	Value	Quantity	Value
	5100	500			1700	1000		
					14.700	8100		
			5300	5900	124.400	68.500		
R	400	100			400	200		
	5500	600	5300	5900	141.200	77.800		
	39.400	5500	71.000	79.300	3600	1700		
			900	1300	66.700	40.200		
			7700	8600				
					17.200	10.700		
	9400	1500						
+A								
	4500	700	100	200	500	200		
	900	100	3300*	5800*	62.600	49.500		
			36.800	51.200				
WI								
	54.200	7800	119.800	146.400	150.600	102.300		

TOTAL IMPORTS OF RAW MATERIA

Total imports for NATO-countries 1960	8		9		10	
	Crude rubber		Iron ore		Lead ore	
Countries of origin	Quantity	Value	Quantity	Value	Quantity	Value
CENTRAL AMERICA						
Guatamala					4000	100
Honduras					1000	30
Nicaragua						
Mexico				500	30.600	610
Dominican Rep.			100	1000		
Total			100	1500	35.600	740
SOUTH AMERICA						
Argentinia						
Bolivia					13.900	230
Brazil	2700	2700	2600*	58.500*		
Chile			600*	39.200*	5800	70
Colombia						
Ecuador						
Br. Guiana						
Fr. Guiana						
Surinam + Ant.	200	300				
Paraguay						
Peru	200	100	1600*	48.700*	67.100	12.50
Uruguay						
Venezuela	200	300	4300*	199.300*		
French West Indies						
Total	3300	3400	9100	345.700	86.800	15.50

* Excl. the U.S.

38

R N.A.T.O.-COUNTRIES

| | 11 | | 12 | | 13 | | 14 | |
| | Zinc ore | | Manganese ore | | Silver and Platinum ores | | Copper (unwrought) | |
	Quantity	Value	Quantity	Value	Quantity	Value	Quantity	Value
	2100	200						
	3200	700						
R	184.700	13.600					8800*	8700
	190.000	14.500	184.700	13.600			8800	8700
o	20.400	900						
r	5900	500			1078			
h			333.000	26.000			298.500*	225.000
o								
G								
G								
+A								
a								
e	182.500	13.900			2850		59.800*	47.400
WI								
	208.800	15.300	333.000	26.000	3928		358.300	272.400

TOTAL IMPORTS OF RAW MATERIA

| Total imports for NATO-countries 1960 | 15 | | 16 | | 17 | |
| | Nickel (unwrought) | | Aluminium (unwrought) | | Tin (unwrought) | |
Countries of origin	Quantity	Value	Quantity	Value	Quantity	Value
CENTRAL AMERICA						
Guatemala						
Honduras						
Nicaragua						
Mexico						
Dominican Rep.						
Total						
SOUTH AMERICA						
Argentinia						
Bolivia						1000	200
Brazil						
Chile						
Colombia						
Ecuador						
Br. Guiana						
Fr. Guiana						
Surinam + Ant.						
Paraguay						
Peru						
Uruguay						
Venezuela						
French West Indies						
Total					1000	200

† Excl. Canada.
* Excl. the U.S.

40

R N.A.T.O.-COUNTRIES

	18 Lead (unwrought)		19 Zinc (unwrought)		20 Petroleum (unwrought)		21 Inorganic chemicals	
	Quantity	Value	Quantity	Value	Quantity	Value	Quantity	Value
R	47.700†*	25.700	16.800	4300	100	1400	500	3000
	47.700	25.700	16.800	4300	100	1400	500	3000
					100	1400	1000	400
					4500	78.100	23.700	4400
j					1000†	29.000		
j					1500	28.600		
- A	37.600†*	13.600	16.400	6800	200	5100		
					46.300	918.800		
VI								
	37.600	13.600	16.400	6800	53.600	1061.000	24.700	4800

nations and still more to their political independence of Communist influence. The military balance of power we were talking about in the Introduction will be influenced both by our production capacity and by having at our disposal the required quantities and assortment of raw materials in the underdeveloped countries. Therefore safeguarding peace depends to a high degree on the availability of raw materials.

In connexion with raw materials we may conclude that the underdeveloped countries are able to influence our peace as well as our war economy, and this justifies our interest in the underdeveloped world and makes it necessary for us to give aid and technical assistance to them.

Let us now have a look at the other side of the problems with respect to the non-committed nations. The standard of living of a people not only influences the type of economy developed by a nation but indicates also its economic activity.

From a military point of view a large population has in itself a certain interest as it is usually considered to be an asset and for that reason a positive factor in the balance of power. Technological progress resulting in increased mechanization in modern warfare has made the size of the population less important than in the past. When total production per capita is increasing, it is much easier to build up a strong defence system. Increase in population and a rise in per capita production are both important aspects of the total of the economic growth of a nation. A rapid growth of the population today is likely to make an advanced nation more vulnerable. Man is not only a consumer, but also a factor of production and in the latter respect we are only interested in the number of people fit to work. An increase of the labour force may result in an increase of production and a general rise in the standard of living. However, this will only occur when an output is achieved which exceeds the national consumption including that of all the people not yet or no longer taking part in production or delivery of services (children, retired people, housewives, etc.).

Generally speaking, most of the N.A.T.O. countries have gained prosperity as a result of research, technological progress, accelerated industrialization, good management and an adequate sales organization. Mass-production may result in a lowering of costs and selling prices, but markets have to be developed to get rid of the huge amount of produced items. A rise of income per capita facilitates the sale within the national region, but mass-production and specialization necessitate a stimulation of exports in order to lower the cost. On the other hand mass-production and mechanization will lower the demand for labour and only a widening of the assortment of consumer goods and increased exports will prevent unemployment, and also a lowering of income per capita. The economic situation will be different in the various regions and nations. Let us have a short look at the economic prospects within N.A.T.O. and start with Europe.

As we have seen, there will probably be only a relatively small increase in the population of the European countries of N.A.T.O. The tendency to an increase in the older age groups as a natural corollary of the declining death-rate, combined with the desire to reduce the working hours and an extension of holidays, will produce a certain negative rate of growth of the labour force, in terms of hours of work and production. This means that it will only be possible to achieve an increase in the net domestic product in total as well as per capita by rising productivity. This rise will only be obtained by an increase of real capital and improvement of capital equipment. The available resources in Western Europe have already been fairly exhaustively exploited. Therefore our dependence on imports of raw materials, as we mentioned before, is increasing. To pay for these imports and to prevent unemployment, as well as to maintain income per capita, Western Europe has to export a huge number and a large assortment of manufactured goods. It will be clear that the way in which the backward nations, which produce the major raw materials, develop, is very important for Western Europe, as a considerable part of the economic activities of Western Europe is based on imports of raw materials. Western Europe has to pay for these raw materials. For that reason Western Europe has to export manufactured goods, but that means also the necessity of having and creating markets outside Europe, where an increasing percentage of the manufactured goods can be sold.

There already exists a considerable foreign trade among the Western countries. But in connexion with the import of raw materials, there can be little doubt that future economic growth of the European N.A.T.O. region will largely depend on the trend of development in the countries of the free world that produce raw materials. Therefore Africa, Asia and Latin America will become more and more important trading partners for Europe.

Figures I, II and III show the size and density of a number of nations in various regions of the free world (with a population of more than 9 million people) and in connexion with the expected growth of the population in Asia, Africa and Latin America (Table I) it will be clear that these regions will develop into very important markets for West European manufactured goods. Also we have to bear in mind the aspiration for a further rise of income per capita in Europe. This will increase the demand for capital and consumer goods, but will also

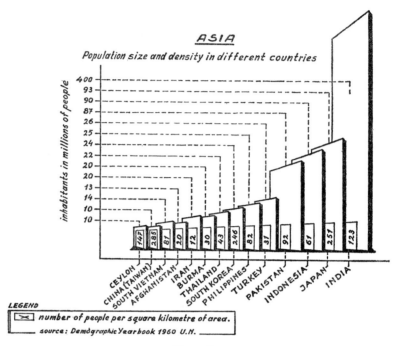

Figure I

result in turn in a rise of the imports of raw materials. Higher income per capita requires higher output of the labour force, lowering of the costs of manufacturing by increased mass-production, and also intensification of applied research and development.

It will be clear that the European N.A.T.O. countries will only be able to maintain or promote prosperity and also maintain an adequate defence, if the trend of increasing exports is not interrupted. The European region of N.A.T.O., as will now be readily understood, is anxious to build up new markets in the underdeveloped countries. Today these countries are having serious payment problems and it is understandable that Western Europe has a considerable interest in giving aid and technical assistance to the backward nations. There will come a time when the underdeveloped countries will show an increasing demand for manufactured goods. The Soviets are well aware of the dependence of the European N.A.T.O. countries on the underdeveloped world, both for their prosperity and fight against unemployment and for the preservation of the West European defence against Communist aggression.

Among the conditions influencing the rate of economic growth of Western Europe are the terms of trade. We may not be wrong in

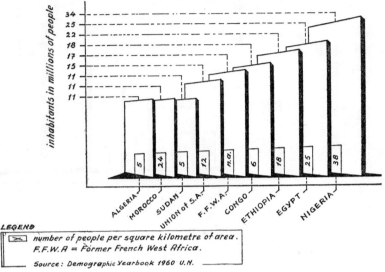

AFRICA

Population size and density in different countries

inhabitants in millions of people

34
25
22
18
17
15
11
11
11

5 2.4 5 1.2 n.a. 6 18 25 38

ALGERIA MOROCCO SUDAN UNION of S.A. F.F.W.A. CONGO ETHIOPIA EGYPT NIGERIA

LEGEND
number of people per square kilometre of area.
F.F.W.A = Former French West Africa.
Source: Demographic Yearbook 1960 U.N.

Figure II

our expectations that in the future the further intensified demand—
resulting in an increased exploitation of natural resources in the underdeveloped countries—will cause a rise in the prices of raw materials.
The integration of the economies of the West European countries
will facilitate to a certain extent the economic problems of the future.
The purpose of the Common Market is mainly the realization of the
advantages of increased specialization and the use of the most modern
production techniques. All this will result in an improvement of the
terms of trade. It is desirable but also necessary to extend the Common
Market to all the European N.A.T.O. countries, or still better, to
the whole of free Western Europe. The stronger the West European
economy, the less will be the chance that the U.S.S.R. will decide on
military aggression. Unified Western Europe will be a more powerful
unit, increase economic stability, ensure continuous expansion, and
raise the income per capita, and the attainment of these ends should
result in prosperity both for Western Europe and for the underdeveloped world.

Now let us have a look at the other side of the Atlantic. The U.S.A.
and Canada have excellent resources of fertile land and raw materials,
both of which will be sufficient for the near future.

Both are dependent for only a small number of raw materials on
other countries.

Population size and density in different countries

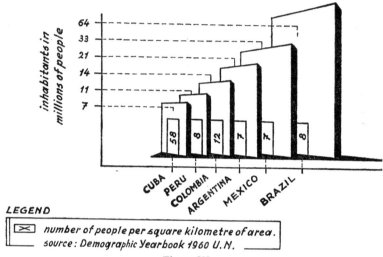

LEGEND

⊠ number of people per square kilometre of area.
source: Demographic Yearbook 1960 U.N.

Figure III

Nevertheless, the United States of America, and also Canada to a certain extent, will have to face some problems which must not be underestimated. In the U.S.A. we can expect a big increase in the productive age groups within 10 to 15 years. At the moment there is already unemployment (seasonally adjusted 5.4% in the U.S.A. and 7.5% in Canada) and therefore the availability of labour will continue to be a matter of serious concern to the U.S.A. government. Reduction of working hours and extension of holidays have not yet resulted in a decrease of unemployment. Lowering of the age of retirement may be one of the solutions. The growth of population will result in higher consumption, but it is questionable if this will be of high importance for the problem of unemployment. There is a tendency in the U.S.A. to raise wages, anticipating an increase of output and furthermore this raising of wages may promote gradually a less material attitude of life, creating in turn a demand for more leisure time, resulting in a delay in the economic growth. The employers may be reluctant, as a result of these attitudes towards an easier way of living, to increase the number of employees, trying to meet the increased demand for manufactured goods by more mechanization and better management in order to prevent a further rise of cost prices. Although for the time being the U.S.A. has a high degree of independence in regard to prosperity and economic growth, it has not been possible to avoid unemployment. If the rise of national consumption is not able to solve this problem, there will be a need for expansion of foreign trade. In spite of the very high wages in the U.S.A. in comparison with those in the other advanced countries of the world, reduction of costs, among other things by mass-production, has made it possible up to now to maintain competitive prices on the world market. Already the U.S.A. is feeling the effect of the Common Market and the situation will get worse if other European countries too join the Common Market. The Common Market will result in a decrease of cost prices of the European products, among other things by increased specialization and mass-production.

Therefore, the American exports to Western Europe will be affected unfavourably and this will force the U.S.A. to look out for other markets to sell its manufactured goods. Both the U.S.A. and Western Europe are now highly industrialized and specialized, also manufacturing to a large extent the same kinds of products; therefore competition on the European market will become an increasingly hard job for the U.S.A. In my opinion there is every reason for the U.S.A. to pay full attention to the underdeveloped countries as future markets for American goods in order to make up for their dwindling positions on the West European market.

I do not think we have to fear a serious and devastating competition between Western Europe and North America in the free underdeveloped world, as the needs there are still so high that for the next few decades the demand will never be met. I am sure that there will come into being an agreement between North America and Western Europe to avoid a devastating competition in order to capture the markets in the underdeveloped free world. Historical ties between the advanced nations and certain regions or countries (Commonwealth, Communauté, inter-American relations, etc.) will also play an important role in the division of markets. There may also be other reasons justifying but also forcing the U.S.A. to pay increased attention to the backward nations, and these are based on financial considerations. All I want to prove, examining the economy of the U.S.A., is the necessity for the Americans to obtain increased export possibilities in the underdeveloped countries.

The central and basic problem of the U.S. economy is an external one. The balance of payments has been developed in the wrong direction; we learn that since 1950 the deficits on overall account grew steadily, resulting in a crisis in the dollar position in 1960. Most experts have tried to find the causes of this disturbance in the capital sector of the balance of payments. According to a recent investigation into the causes and issues of the balance of payments problem, the most important shift did not take place in the capital sector but in that of the balance of trade. Looking at the figures of the years 1957— 1959 we see that the amount of exports over imports decreased during this period. Although a thorough investigation of the international competitive strength of the U.S. manufactured products has not been made up to now, there is every reason to expect that especially owing to the development of the relative labour cost, the U.S.A. may face big problems in this field for the near future.

In the U.S.A. the wages, salaries and social cost per head have risen faster than the labour-productivity per capita in the industrial sector. This cost inflation has resulted in a price inflation both for domestic market products and for export products. Although in some European countries (France and United Kingdom) similar price inflations can be seen, it is probable that in the U.S.A. this tendency has caused more trouble than in Europe. We must not forget that in the U.S.A. the governmental price- and employment policy is still based on monetary and budgetary means. In the majority of the West European countries the wages have been controlled during the last few years, owing to a sensible agreement between governments, employers and trade-unions, which has shown extremely good results especially in the Netherlands, but also in France and Germany. Up to now there has not been set up in the U.S.A. a centralized and co-ordinated wage policy equal to that existing in Western Europe (especially in the Netherlands). One of the most important means of economic policy—the wage- and salary level and structure—has been neglected in the U.S.A. with all the inflationary results thereof.

Other factors, too, have worked to the detriment of the U.S. competitive strength and the balance of payments situation. I must mention here:

a. shifts in the consumption of American to European industrial products of high quality;

b. too big investments in some major industries in the U.S.A. (car and aircraft production);

c. import restrictions on American goods in most of the European countries in the initial period after the war;

d. increase of the flow of private American capital to Europe, in anticipation of higher profit rates;

e. the European economic integration resulting in shrinking costs of production.

I am sure that the only way to solve the balance of payments problems of the U.S.A. is an attempt to overcome the competitive

48

power of Western Europe by pricing the American products very sharply and above all by creating new markets in the underdeveloped nations.

Both the U.S.A. (and Canada) and the European N.A.T.O. countries are confronted with the poverty of the backward nations and are willing to give them aid and technical assistance in order not to drive them into the arms of the Communists. A reduction in the aid to the underdeveloped countries to solve the U.S. balance of payments problems may result in a very dangerous and undesirable political situation.

I hope I have made it clear that there is every reason to speak of an economic vulnerability of most of the N.A.T.O. nations and consequently of N.A.T.O. as a whole.

In my opinion the two factors—the raw materials and the new markets—as explained above, influencing to such a large extent our peace economy, but likewise or perhaps still more our strategic economic war-potential, are today so indissolubly linked with the majority of the more or less underdeveloped nations. Also taking into account the increasing economic threat by the U.S.S.R., they must engage our most serious attention in N.A.T.O. I would like to repeat that "the balance of deterrence", meant to force the U.S.S.R. to renounce any idea of local or large-scale aggression, will lose much of its value unless the economic situation in the whole of N.A.T.O. is healthy and able to support the required expenditures for the military defence.

Mr. D. U. Stikker, Secretary General of N.A.T.O. in a speech delivered at the opening ceremony of the Ministerial Meeting at Athens on May 4, 1962, declared that the Communist threat is worldwide and that the threat to which this pressure subjects us is a constant one, which manifests itself all over the earth and which assumes all possible forms, of which the political and economic are certainly the most pernicious. Such a state of affairs imposes duties on us and dictates our line of conduct for the future. He finished with the following statement: "In the economic field, we must, moreover, expand our resources at a rate which will not only enable us to meet the expense entailed by the maintenance and strengthening of our military capabilities, but also to safeguard the social balance and the domestic political stability of the member countries whose peoples must also enjoy higher living standards.

Last, but not least, we must concern ourselves with the economic welfare of the so-called "underdeveloped" countries which have only recently acquired their independence.

A big effort in this direction has already been undertaken by the countries of the free world. But we must make sure that this effort in favour of the less fortunate countries continues to be intensified. N.A.T.O. has responsibilities in this field".[8]

8. N.A.T.O. Press Release M1(62)3.

CHAPTER III

THOUGHTS ABOUT WESTERN POLICY
IN THE COLD WAR

There is no peace or war between East and West, but we are living in a situation in which we are continuously forced to safeguard our existence and to take our safety precautions. We must fully realize the manifold world-wide and unlimited character of the Communist offensive against N.A.T.O. and also that the economic threat of the Soviets fits in very well with the cold war. In the military field—although not with complete satisfaction—we are able to maintain a balance of deterrence, just enough to enable us to suppose that it will do to prevent Soviet aggression.

However, N.A.T.O.'s economic position is vulnerable as we explained in the previous chapter. If we had all the required means in our own hands to strengthen our economies and to maintain prosperity, just as we do with military defence, we could estimate the exact risk we are facing in regard to the economic competition between the Soviet bloc and N.A.T.O. At present the underdeveloped nations are controlling up to a point some of the essential tools of our economies; however, that does not mean that they will decide on our future.

It is up to the Western world to decide on the chances of a rapid economic growth of the underdeveloped countries and on the level of prosperity they will attain. If the Western world is on good terms with the underdeveloped countries, we both will have the benefit of that. In spite of our gradual dependence on the underdeveloped nations, we still are in a much stronger position than they. We may be handicapped by a lack of some essential raw materials, although we may be able to develop artificial substitutes or may lose our prosperity to a certain degree by losing foreign markets for our manufactured goods. The underdeveloped nations are in a worse position as they would be deprived of the aid they need for their economic growth. One may say that the U.S.S.R. and Communist China will be quite willing to give them aid. However, the Communist bloc itself has only one alternative, viz. between an economic growth, enabling the Communists to catch up with and overtake N.A.T.O. in per capita output of goods, or a retardation in economic growth as a result of a huge aid programme to help the underdeveloped world. If the

Table V

INEQUALITY BETWEEN RICH AND POOR COUNTRIES

Countries	Population in millions	National income in milliard dollars	Per capita national income in dollars
I. 16 Highly developed countries with capitalistic structure	385	536	1,390
II. Soviet Union and other not so highly developed European countries	450	198	440
III. Latin America	195	41	210
IV. Africa, Oceania (excluding New Zealand and Australia). Asia (excluding Soviet Union)	1,800	195	108
Total:	2,830	970	342

Source: "De Malthus à Mao Tsé-Toung", Alfred Sauvy, p. 138.

Kremlin's long-term plan for the engulfment of the free world depends upon both, the preservation of rate of growth narrowing or overwhelming the gap in economic power and prosperity between the Communist world and N.A.T.O. and also to represent an attraction to lure the backward nations within its orbit, then the Communists will be forced to accept a retardation for decades of their political aim of world domination. The result of a slowing-down of the Communist aid to the backward nations will not stimulate the sympathy for the Communist doctrines or be an attractive example of the Communist paradise. Up till now the West has been able to offer the underdeveloped nations a much better chance to grow to economic maturity and most of the leaders of the newly independent nations are well aware of that. Table V shows the inequality between rich and poor countries. It will be clear that the U.S.S.R., even assisted by Communist China, will never be able—considering their own internal economic problems and their weakness in the field of manufacturing of consumer goods—to compete with the aid and technical assistance of the size the Western world has given to the underdeveloped countries. However, the prospect for increased internal trade in capital goods between the backward nations must not be underestimated too much. The interest of the Communists in trading with the underdeveloped countries is twofold. First, for N.A.T.O. it would mean a merciless competitor on the markets of the underdeveloped world. Already we have a foretaste of what we may expect. The Soviets are providing Italy and other countries with oil at a price only just over half (52%) the corresponding price Soviet satellites are charged. This proves it is not at all impossible that other Soviet products, too, may be sold to any country in the free world at "political prices". As the U.S.S.R. is utterly inimical to N.A.T.O. and will subordinate commercial interest to political ends, we may not be wrong to expect a devastating competition on the markets of the underdeveloped world, if that would suit Soviet political aims in order to undermine the N.A.T.O. economies. Competition on the markets of the free world is reasonable as long as the prices are determined by considerations of demand and supply and competition in each particular market. As soon as dumping takes place—based on political motives—the situation will worsen. In regard to the vulnerability of the economies of the N.A.T.O. countries and our necessity to develop markets for our manufactured goods, we will not be able to compete with the Communists using "political prices". Any discussion on economic relations between the Communists and N.A.T.O. respectively, and the underdeveloped world, has to take into account that we are dealing with a delicate problem where political and economic factors and influences are closely interlocked. The demand for consumer goods in the U.S.S.R. is increasing and may lead to the conclusion that there is no cause for undue anxiety. Heavy industry—the production of capital goods—has always been mollycoddled by the Communist leaders and the Soviets have already delivered a lot of capital goods to underdeveloped countries. How much priority will the Soviets give to developing trade in capital goods with the backward nations, as distinct from a concentration of all their resources on internal growth? Let us not overlook the fact that the underdeveloped countries have more interest in machinery than in consumer goods. Second, also not in favour of N.A.T.O., may be the fact that Soviet machinery is less complicated than ours. Handling, maintenance and repair of the Soviet machineries demands less education and technical training. Technological progress in the U.S.S.R. has led to the production of more complicated machines, just as we saw in the recent past in the West. Therefore the U.S.S.R. may replace the obsolescent machineries by the most modern equipment and sell these old machineries at "political prices" to the underdeveloped nations without disturbing the Communist technical and economic growth. On the contrary, the sale of obsolescent or even obsolete machineries may be an extra profit for the Soviet economy and balance of payments. The underdeveloped countries, just by reason of their lack of technically skilled workers, may prefer the less complicated machineries to the highly complicated Western capital goods. In this regard it may be interesting to cite Alec Nove: "When the re-equipment of Soviet agriculture is further advanced, there may be surplus capacity, available for export, in the tractor and other farm machinery industries. Some other well-developed engineering sectors (perhaps machine-tools or excavators) could provide a surplus, but the whole question of machinery exports is bound up with uncertainties about internal requirements"[9] The re-equipment of soviet agriculture will definitely free obsolete material, which will nevertheless be of value to the more or less primitive agriculture of a considerable number of backward countries.

The U.S.S.R. may export obsolete, obsolescent and even new farm machineries to the backward nations and that means an influence on N.A.T.O. export possibilities. Perhaps we should do well not to take this export to backward nations too lightly, as the demand in the underdeveloped nations is enormous.

I think that in regard to political and economic matters we must not be too short-sighted, especially not as the Soviet plans for the near future are very ambitious. The uncommitted nations will have to pay for the goods they are buying from the Communists and therefore they have to finance these imports by selling raw materials and agricultural products to the U.S.S.R. If the Soviets are willing to sell their products very cheap—and they will do so in some cases from a political point of view—the backward nations may conclude that the Western countries are trying to exploit them by asking higher prices. We in N.A.T.O. may also have obsolete or obsolescent machineries, still of high value for the underdeveloped countries and I think we will do well to give these goods away instead of selling them or throwing them away. It is a form of aid that will obtain goodwill, but will also take the wind out of the Communists' sails. In this respect we are absolutely able to outbid the Russians.

The U.S.S.R. has increased the tempo and scope of its trade promotion drive. A lot of trade missions have been sent out, pressing for conclusion of trade agreements and stressing expanded trade. In most cases the Soviets are taking a very firm stand and everything they do, whether giving or loaning, will take place on a bilateral basis. The money they have made available to the underdeveloped nations must be spent in the Communist sphere. The West is giving aid partly on a multilateral basis and in consequence the ties between the West and the uncommitted nations are not so close as they could be.

We are forgetting too often that we are involved in a cold war, in which the economic factor is playing a role of steadily increasing im-

9. Alec Nove and Desmond Donnelly, Trade with Communist Countries, London 1960, p. 50.

portance. In such a severe competition there is no place for excessive ethical arguments.

Both the U.S.S.R. and N.A.T.O.-countries are developing so rapidly as a result of the technological progress that the gap between them and the underdeveloped world is widening more and more. This is a very depressing fact for the underdeveloped nations. However, when the aid from an advanced country to a developing or really backward nation is well planned and worked out in the interests of both of them, the gap in economic growth will narrow instead of widening. Although we are used to comparing the economic potential of the U.S.S.R. with ours, we also have to take into account the economic potential of the European satellites of Russia. Many of the East European nations have a considerable manufacturing power, but also a notable commercial experience. Therefore in respect of foreign trade with the uncommitted nations they may operate much more effectively than the Soviets. It is remarkable that the Soviet bloc as a whole has scarcely made an impact on the backward nations as a market for their exports and as a source for raw materials. Most activity in this field has taken place on a bilateral basis between one of the European satellites and one of the uncommitted countries. It is true that the Soviet bloc is self-sufficient to a high degree in relation to raw materials (about 98%). However, we must envisage a rapid growth of the economy of the U.S.S.R. as well as a better organization in regard to foreign trade by the Soviet bloc as a whole. That progress may have a certain influence on the self-sufficiency in relation to some raw materials.

The time will come when the Soviet bloc will pay more attention to the manufacturing of consumer goods and later on to the export of them. A rise in prosperity in the Soviet bloc will definitely result in a less aggressive attitude towards the West. Nevertheless, even a manifold increase in Communist foreign trade will not alter the fact that the economies of the underdeveloped nations will continue to be interwoven with the trade of N.A.T.O. It will be a hard, if not an impossible task for the Communists to beat the West in manufacturing capacity.

Although I do not want to overrate the importance of the Communist productive capacity, I would like to warn against too much wishful thinking in this respect.

In an article "Russia's claims debunked" in U.S. News and World Report of May 2, 1960, we are told that the U.S.S.R. is, in relation to the U.S.A., 19 years behind in steel production, 36 years in the production of trucks and busses, 49 years in the manufacturing of cars and so on. Furthermore Russia with inefficient farming methods uses nearly ten times as many people as the U.S.A. to do farmwork. The

Soviet railway system has a length of just 6% of that of the U.S.A. All these figures seek to prove that we need not fear the economic potential of the U.S.S.R. and that the Soviet achievements that have impressed the world are mostly in a few narrow fields—such as weapons and heavy industry—into which tremendous effort has been poured by a ruthless dictatorship.

Let us now go back to the steel production of the U.S.S.R. and the U.S.A. At first sight we may be very satisfied. However, when we look at the quantities of steel that both the U.S.S.R. and the U.S.A. are using for the production of railway material, heavy machinery, tanks, military trucks and so on, we see practically no difference. That means that in the production of heavy military equipment or goods of strategic economic value, there is no difference. The amount of steel which the U.S.A. is using for the manufacturing of consumer goods is very high, but these quantities have nothing to do with the strategic economic war potential or influencing the balance of military power. All I want to prove is that the planned increase in the steel production in the U.S.S.R., as a result of the Seven Year Plan, may be used either for heavy military equipment and the heavy industries or for the production of consumer goods. In the latter case, the internal consumption in the U.S.S.R. may increase without weakening the war potential and in the case of a still larger steel production, consumer goods may also be manufactured for export to the underdeveloped countries. Therefore I am not so sure that in the not too distant future we shall not have to face more competition in capital and consumer goods between the Communists and the West on the markets of the underdeveloped world. In this respect the Soviet satellites may play a very important role! It also means an increased interest of the Communists in the uncommitted nations on purely commercial grounds.

In terms of the political and economic objective of keeping the underdeveloped nations uncommitted or still better in a good relationship with the West—in this way safeguarding the possibilities of foreign trade with them—we have to help them in their desire for economic growth by aid and technical assistance. We have to guide the underdeveloped nations along paths, economic and political, which will ensure that our trade with them shall develop to our mutual benefit, for they are the great markets of the future. This is perhaps in line with our historic colonial mission, but now freed from the exercise of colonial power. This must not be regarded as a form of neo-colonialism but is the logical result of the aim to promote the reciprocal economic interests of the advanced and the underdeveloped nations. In this regard we cannot neglect the interdependence of the economies of all nations in our relatively shrinking world. Today, more than ever before, economic motives and potentialities are a unique and overriding determinant of the course of history. Many underdeveloped nations, proud of their newly won sovereignty, fear to get involved in the controversy between East and West and are over-sensitive in this respect. Therefore we have to proceed in a way that would at least not create hostility against us. On the other hand, regarding our economic vulnerability and some strategic motives, we may be forced to make a distinction—since we have decided to give aid to backward nations—between those that will become firm friends of the West, without affecting their sovereignty and independence in any form—and those only accepting aid but reluctant to grant that foreign trade is profitable for both parties. There is no sense at all in wasting our money on underdeveloped nations, which show a definite hostility against the West and applaud the Communist system and doctrine. On account of our economic vulnerability and the necessity to promote foreign trade with the underdeveloped nations, we must simply concentrate most of our aid and technical assistance, showing our willingness to create a peaceful world without political, military or economic threats. If some of the underdeveloped nations should decide to build up a closer link with the West and especially with the N.A.T.O. countries, we must show our gratitude for such an attitude by further increased aid. The motivation for such an attitude may be based on the supposition that the Communists will not respect their independence and freedom and the fact that they do not have an adequate defence at their disposal.

Another motivation of the underdeveloped nations may be the anticipation of an unshackled economic growth, realizing that the West has more sources available for aid and technical assistance. The West will not have the slightest objection to giving aid in the form of food on a multilateral basis—particularly through the channels of the United Nations—to the hungry people in any backward nation not belonging to the Communist bloc. Some countries will have no objection to this aid on ethical grounds, even though the country belongs to the Communist camp. The same may be true of medical assistance to fight epidemics.

In my opinion all other forms of aid, such as grants, soft loans or technical assistance must be given—using our own Western channels for that purpose (multilateral or bilateral)—to those underdeveloped nations supporting and subscribing to the principles of freedom, self-determination and international trade.

Western aid must be based on sound economic principles. We are vulnerable in our economic existence and therefore we have to do all that will safeguard our economies. Aid on ethical grounds will not be of any value in view of the economic threat used by the U.S.S.R. as a political tool in the cold war.

The strategic economic purpose of our aid is threefold; first we want to safeguard the regular flow of the raw materials we need for our industries; secondly we are creating markets for our products by increasing the economic growth of the underdeveloped countries in order to prevent unemployment of our labour force and bringing prosperity to the people of the underdeveloped world and lastly we are interested in the independence of a few new nations of strategic importance through their geographic location.

The U.S.S.R. has threatened the West with an economic contest and therefore we have to use all our resources in the most efficient way. Our policy in aiding the underdeveloped world has to be realistic and fruitful, serving the interests of the uncommitted nations and of ourselves.

Our freedom and independence, our prosperity and our economic existence in time of cold and hot war are all dependent on our manner of aiding the underdeveloped world and the use we make of our sources of power.

Some people, and in this case I refer to the first part of the book by J. S. Berliner, are of the opinion that the West must channel all its aid through the international agencies of the United Nations. They think, that the more recourse we have to multilateral aid, using the United Nations as mediator, the greater will be the pressure on the U.S.S.R. to do the same. If they continue to refuse, it will become increasingly difficult for the Russians to reconcile their almost exclusive reliance on bilateral aid with their professions of non-interference. If our example led the Soviet Union to channel more of its aid into international agencies, the free world's fears of the implications of Soviet aid would be greatly and properly reduced.[10]

I do not at all subscribe to this wishful thinking. Both the political aim of world domination and the uninterrupted Soviet activities in the cold war between East and West are facts that we cannot by-pass or belittle. The Communists' systems and doctrines will never be given up in order to switch over to ethical motivation. The Communists are as hard as nails in their policy. They want to see political results of their aid and already they have shown that aid is given only to those underdeveloped countries where the political situation holds out a hope for the Communists of gaining ground or setting up a future pro-Communist regime. The Soviet bloc, in the face of its own struggle

10. J. C. Berliner, Soviet Economic Aid, London, 1960.

for economic growth, has to obtain a maximum result out of the funds made available for aid to the underdeveloped nations, and that maximum will only be reached by bilateral aid programs. When we compare the size of the grants to the underdeveloped world, both of the Soviet bloc and the West, there is no doubt that the West is surpassing the Communists enormously. Therefore we must never take the risk that the underdeveloped countries might lose sight of our sincere and so well-demonstrated wish to help them. The Soviets are continually maintaining in the sessions of the United Nations that they are defending the freedom of the uncommitted nations and that they are willing to help them, but they do not implement their promises by giving increased aid. Assistance through the channels of the United Nations would give the Communists a chance to influence the distribution of aid to the various nations, thereby favouring those countries where political success for Communism is guaranteed. It also gives a chance to the Communists on a much larger scale to infiltrate, under cover of the flag of the United Nations, those backward nations where till now Communism has hardly had a chance.

The West must use its own channels—multilateral or bilateral—to give aid to the uncommitted nations. All we have to do is not to hurt the feeling of the new nations or give them the idea that we would like to influence their internal affairs. We need not hide the necessity of close co-operation between the West and the new nations for the benefit of both. We want to treat them as equal partners and to show that we only want the programs for aid and technical assistance to be well planned, but also wish to ensure that the money made available to them will be spent in the proper and most effective way in order to speed up their economic growth.

In the cold war weakness, ethical motives and carelessness have no sense and no value. Western aid to the underdeveloped countries has to be founded on a realistic policy, taking into account our military and strategic economic interests.

Today the emotions created by the slogans of nationalism are often so over-excited as to cause the West to get confused in respect to its principal aim. Some political philosophers try to tell us in their misleading and imposing books that the business of the West is to ensure the greatest good to the greatest number; welfare, health, freedom, justice, peace, and so on. In their train of thought, we in the West are the only people who have to play the role of the benefactor of the underdeveloped world. However—N.A.T.O. being threatened by the Communists—our main political aim is to safeguard our own existence and freedom. If the aid to the underdeveloped countries fits well into the whole complex of measures we have to take for the purpose of

Western defense, so much the better. There is not the slightest objection to giving a part of our prosperity to those people on earth still going hungry throughout their lives, but is does not mean that we have to ignore our self-interest and the immense advantage of freedom to all, based on the Western defence. The former colonial powers need not have a feeling of guilt, pressed upon them by the Communist propaganda or by fanatical leaders of some new nations.

I would like to draw attention to the fact, that countries such as Ethiopia and Liberia, being independent since 1896 and 1847 respectively, although possessing considerable natural resources, hardly show a more rapid increase in economic progress and prosperity. Therefore independence does not always mean that the nations are better off as soon as they are able to look after their own affairs. They were fighting the same problems as the new nations of today, but lacked the capital and technical assistance all underdeveloped countries need from the advanced societies. A look at table I shows the population growth of the underdeveloped world; such a growth in former colonies would never have taken place if the colonial powers had not done their best to combat against dreadful pestilences there. Of course, we could have done more, but it should never be overlooked that only in the last few decades the West has reached a level of prosperity, enabling it to help others to a larger extent. I really do not have to describe the poverty that in the past ruled in the slums of the industrial towns, and likewise in some agricultural areas of Europe, to prove the impossibility of substantial aid programmes to the colonies in those days. Nobody can deny that the new nations now have at their disposal road and railway networks, well equiped harbours, schools and so on, built by their former colonial rulers.

Today, in the interest of N.A.T.O. defence, we are increasing our aid to the underdeveloped world, but on ethical grounds we are even doing much more in this regard.

There are in fact two recent and important developments in our divided world of today. First, colonialism has practically come to an end. Figure IV shows the situation in the world in 1959 with regard to the people still living under a colonial regime, in contrast with the majority of the world's people living in freedom. Since 1959 still more countries have become independent and also those few left under the colonial regime will obtain freedom sooner or later. The whole problem of aid to the underdeveloped world is not an easy one. Practice has shown that nationalist passion has become sometimes the greatest enemy of national interest, justice and prosperity. This holds good especially for the new independent nations, giving preference to a complete cutting off all the ties with the former colonial countries and chasing

60

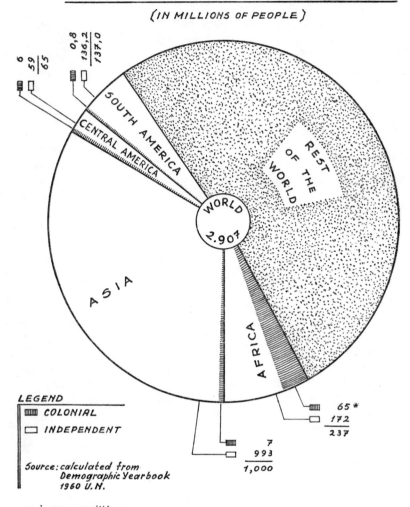

POPULATION AND POLITICAL STATUS OF THE WORLD 1959

(IN MILLIONS OF PEOPLE)

Figure IV

away all the former colonists. The latter could have been their best advisers, following their experience and knowledge of the country and most of them will be able and willing to accept the new conditions under which they will have to work in the new independent nation. Also their experience may be of high value if it were to be used in other new nations with more or less similar climatic and social conditions. This is all the more true for the private entrepreneurs, who—

just as in the colonial period—have nothing to do with the governing of the country.

The other development is that poverty has become intolerable to the poor peoples in the backward nations, because they think that it is a holy duty of the advanced countries to give aid and consequently poverty no longer has to be regarded as inevitable. Three-fourths of the world's population lives in poverty and often under unacceptable conditions, whereas the rest is more or less blessed with prosperity. They all want the Good Life for all and they shout the same slogans, none more loudly than the Communists. They do not realize how much effort is needed to obtain a reasonable level of prosperity.

We have only to look at our faithful N.A.T.O. allies—Turkey and Greece—receiving a considerable amount of aid from the West, to understand how time-consuming is the growth to economic progress and maturity. How time-consuming will it be to bring prosperity to even less developed nations, especially when their governments are over-sensitive in regard to the former colonial nations and suspicious in regard to the advisers and the technical assistance of the advanced Western countries. This attitude of some of the new nations will force the West to a very considerate handling of the problem of aid to those underdeveloped countries, resulting irrevocably in a delay of the improvement in their living-conditions and their national economies. We all know that at present no nation need fear a return to colonialism. Any move to return to colonialism would only drive those nations into the arms of the Communists and that is just what we want to prevent at any price. We are giving aid and technical assistance to the free underdeveloped world—as we explained before —because we stand in need of them for our own economic existence and furthermore, with the best intentions of humanity, to lift them out of their primitive and often unbearable living conditions. Although we are giving our aid, based not only on philanthropy but above all on sound economic reasons, this state of things is not a disgrace to N.A.T.O. or the Western world. However, Communist aid is based to the full extent on political motives and there is not the slightest sign of philantropy to be discovered in the Soviet behaviour! It is a pity that the new nations, able to judge for themselves, do not pay full attention to this difference in attitude between East and West. A comparison between the amount of the grants (and the conditions attached to them), given respectively by the Communists and the West, could teach them a lot!

The purpose of a Western programme of aid to underdeveloped countries is to accelerate their economic development up to the point where these new nations are able to look after themselves. The

62

object we have in view when giving aid must not be to raise the standards of living in the recipient nations by a constant and uninterrupted flow of capital or food to them for many years to come, but to permit the new countries to make the transition from economic stagnation to self-sustaining economic growth. We are willing to give them the aid and technical assistance they need, but the populations of the new nations themselves have to use these tools properly. Generally speaking, the aim of our aid is to supply the new nation with a positive incentive for maximum national effort to raise the standards of living but simultaneously to increase and to speed up its rate of economic growth. It has also to be understood by the governments of the new nations that modern government is a very complicated affair and that it will only be for their own benefit if they call upon the more experienced advanced countries for assistance in order to work out the development programs. This assistance will definitely result in an accelerated economic progress. If the governments of the new nations reject the assistance of the advanced countries, the backward countries will fall more and more behind. Technical assistance, aid and private investment provides an opportunity for progress which they can exploit advantageously. The fisherman, the peasant in his rice paddy, the man who makes primitive utensils, household articles or ornaments, have awakened from centuries of lethargy. They know now that hunger and disease are no longer inevitable and that it is possible to create better living conditions.

Modern communications have brought, even to remote villages in the steaming jungle, the idea that a better life is possible for everybody. Although the present world potentialities for progress and fight against disaster are far-reaching, the people of the underdeveloped countries now very often overestimate these potentialities, especially in regard to the time factor. Too many people in the advanced as well as in the new nations have not recognized that development of the backward countries must be thought of in terms of decades. Adequate attention has to be given to investment in education, technical and administrative training, etc. The people have to be taught and trained how to make effective use of the available resources. In the underdeveloped countries there is an immense need for training of all kinds, from on-the-job training of artisans to the more complex sciences of technology and economics. Economic progress will depend to a large extent upon the educational equipment for engineering and scientific training.

We have to respect the national pride of the over-sensitive new nations and to avoid any semblance of superiority, patronage or racial discrimination. On the other hand the new nations have to be well aware of the fact that our aid provides them with an opportunity for progress, which they can either use to their own benefit or throw away. Whatever aid the underdeveloped nations receive, their progress still depends upon their own effort, initiative, dash, behaviour as good citizens, organization and government, but also upon their attitude in connexion with international law and justice. The striving for independence has been world-wide. However, political independence has often been obtained by peoples who are seriously divided among themselves. This disunity within a nation is a serious disadvantage and will retard progress.

Some of the leaders of the new nations are very impatient and they have the idea that it must be possible to attain in a short period the same level of political and economical development as that of the West. They think that the aid given to them by the advanced countries is the panacea and the only condition for a relatively rapid drive to maturity. They do not realize that it took 800 to 900 years to clear the jungle of Central and Northwestern Europe. Wars, movements of capital, and migration were the tools to equalize as much as possible the distinctions in wealth between the various European countries. We all know that the European nations at present are trying to unite and although the differences between them are not quite as big as between the West and the underdeveloped world, it is nevertheless a delicate and time-consuming affair.

In this case we have to do with mature nations, having at their disposal a well-established governmental organization, a considerable economic power and lots of highly educated and skilled people. Then how will it be possible for the underdeveloped nations to grow to maturity in a few decades, lacking this potency? Even with the help of the advanced nations their development will be one of the most difficult tasks of our century.

The attitude of the West in connexion with the underdeveloped countries finds expression in speeches made by two well-known authorities.

President Kennedy's remarks at the first national conference of the "Food for Peace Council" on June 28, 1961, were: "As long as there are those who are hungry, it seems to me that we not only have an opportunity but an obligation, particularly here in this rich country, to play our proper role. This is not an element of cold war . . . it is an opportunity which we have because of the generosity of nature and because of the energies of our own people to play in a crucial time in the life of the world an important role in easing and helping the lives of millions of people who are in less fortunate circumstances.[11]

The Secretary General and Chairman of the N.A.T.O. Council, Mr. D. U. Stikker, said at the opening ceremony of the N.A.T.O. Ministerial meeting in Oslo on May 8, 1961, referring to the strategic economic vulnerability of the N.A.T.O. countries in relation to their defence: "The rate of growth of our economies must be such that we can meet the tremendous and growing demand for the maintenance and improvement of our military establishment, while safeguarding and improving the standard of living of our own peoples. In this respect, it seems to me we have a particular interest and a particular obligation to help advance economically the less developed members of our own N.A.T.O. family. But beyond this, we must realize that a great number of nations around the world have a standard of living far below our own. The internal stability and national independence of these countries can only be safeguarded if we, who are more fortunate, are capable of convincing them that we in the West are able and ready, to offer them a better way than the Sino-Soviet bloc, to enable them to increase the productivity of their economies and raise their standard of living"[12]

These two declarations unequivocally state our real and peaceful intentions!

11. For Commanders, This Changing World. The Food for Peace Program, Vol. I no. 13.
12. N.A.T.O.-Press Release M1(61)2.

Chapter IV

PROBLEMS WITH REGARD TO THE UNDERDEVELOPED COUNTRIES

So far we have spoken about the underdeveloped or backward countries, but it will be clear that it is a mistake to use this collective noun for all the new nations. There is a considerable difference in levels of development of the new nations.

Professor W. W. Rostow has identified all societies, in their economic dimensions, as lying within one of five categories: the traditional society, the preconditions for take-off, the take-off, the drive to maturity and the age of high mass-consumption.[13] In my opinion there is also a sixth category, which I would like to call the phase of nuclear energy and computors. That is the economic dimension of our present Western world, wherein atomic energy, the use of all kinds of computors and space travel have paved the way for an accelerated increase of technological and economic progress, widening the gap between the underdeveloped world and the advanced countries. However, on the other hand, this economic dimension may prove to be of value to increase our aid and technical assistance to the nations of a lower category of economic dimension.

It will be clear that there are also other factors influencing the development of a country. Some have a stable and well-established government, a comparatively substantial core of intellectuals and skilled labour, and also already a not too low standard of living, while others are still not far away from the traditional society. In the latter case the only signs of economic growth may be manifested by those few areas where the former colonial power had built up its centres of activity by the creation of towns, harbours, small industries, etc.

Some writers make a comparison between the average annual real income per capita in the advanced countries and in the backward nations. They compare the average real income per capita in the U.S.A. of $ 2000 and in Europe of $ 800 with the $ 120 or still less in the backward nations. Professor Benham, for example, asserts that the size of national income per head of population is the most comprehensive

13. W. W. Rostow, The Stages of Economic Growth, Cambridge, 1960, p. 4.

single measure of the wealth or poverty of a country.[14] Such comparisons are not only misleading but very often tendentious. People living in North America or in Europe have to spend much more money on clothing than those living under tropical conditions. Whereas people in the tropics have to pay just a few pennies and sometimes nothing to obtain vegetables and fruit, those in the advanced countries have to pay much more. The same can be said about the costs of heating. Therefore such comparisons are worthless and will only result in bad feelings on the side of the population of the backward states.

For various reasons we shall never be able to use the same pattern of measures to assist the underdeveloped nations. Therefore it may prove valuable, in respect of our study, to present some more information about the new nations and the characteristics of the various regions of the free world.

The size and density of the population in the different regions and countries are important factors in regard to the chances of economic development and the aid we have to give them. Figures I, II and III, as we showed in chapter II, prove that there is not very much resemblance in their specific character. Some of them with a high number of people per square kilometre of area have a higher income per capita than others with less density of population.

One of the most frightening facts in our world today, and particularly in the underdeveloped nations, is the population explosion. The enormous potential population increase in the underdeveloped nations, induced by Western public health techniques, is one of the main problems of the new nations. Now the new governments are able to lower the death-rate still more by improving the hygienic conditions and medical care—continuing the work done in this field by the former colonial powers—but they cannot keep down the birth-rate. The latter will be possible only if the people themselves are convinced that it is in their own interest. This is the case in Japan. However, in most countries birth control or facilities for abortion still arouse strong opposition on religious grounds. The rapid growth of population in most of the underdeveloped countries will result in serious problems, as usually there is an increasing lag between the economic growth and the growth of population. The underdeveloped nations, already comprising 65.5 per cent of the world population (including Red China), may increase according to recent estimates to 76.3 per cent by the year 2000. How to feed these masses of people is one of the most important problems to solve.

In my opinion there can be no sustained improvement in general

14. Professor F. Benham, Economic aid to underdeveloped countries, London, 1961, p. 3.

living standards in the new nations without an appreciable advance in the agricultural sector. The basic material need of mankind is food! In its present backwardness, agriculture is not only a drag on progress, but in the near future a serious threat to the growth of population. There can be no talk about industrialization as long there is no substantial increase in agricultural production in order to feed the industrial population. In this regard I would like to cite Dr. Saco: "I will conclude by saying that agriculture has a vital part to play in the development process, for the obvious reasons that, without it, the primary food requirements cannot be met. Whatever may be its relative importance in the economy as a whole, productivity must be increased, to permit the creation of capital and the liberation of manpower. This would be essential at any time, but especially in the stage of economic growth described as "take-off", and until the accelerating impulse is transferred to other sectors of economy. I must not conclude without a reference to the vital necessity now existing to pay careful attention to all problems of economic development in general, and to the problems of agricultural progress in particular, if the increasing food requirements of the world population are to be properly met".[15]

Many backward nations have natural advantages of climate or soil which would enable them to increase agricultural production. However, many peasants follow traditional practices instead of adopting improved systems which would result in much higher yields. This may be due to their reluctance to change or to ignorance. Very often, especially in countries where arable land is scarce, many farms are much too small to give a surplus of food for the industrial population and hardly provide an adequate livelihood to the cultivators themselves. In a lot of backward countries we find a multitude of very small farms of 2 to 5 acres, making it impossible to use agricultural machinery.

For the time being the only way to get higher yields from these small farms without high expense is to instruct the peasants on such matters as the better use of facilities, the rotation of crops, the use of improved seeds, better methods of cultivation, construction of a primitive but widespread system of irrigation, soil conservation, better use of livestock, measures to control diseases affecting livestock and crops, etc. In this manner, without mechanization and with relatively low costs, a considerably higher yield can be obtained. Textbook solutions, advocating complete mechanization of agriculture,

15. Dr. A. Saco, Farm productivity and income as related to economic growth, p. 69. Problems of development. (Series of lectures on economic growth, OEEC, 1961.)

are mostly not feasible as a result of the structure of agriculture in the tropical countries. It will take a long time before the governments of the underdeveloped nations are able to enlarge the size of the farms and to offer jobs to those who are no longer required in the modernized agricultural activities. Neither the system of bureaucratic collective farms nor introduction of labour-saving machines will be a solution. It would result in an increased unemployment in the agricultural sector at the very moment when there are still not enough jobs available in other sectors of economic activity. Especially Africa and Asia are facing the problems we have outlined here. We must also observe that life in most of the Asiatic and African underdeveloped countries is very much oriented around the family and these families are mostly very large. The family ties are very strong and tradition plays a very important role. All this will make it very difficult to enlarge the size of the farms. Also the tribes in Africa—in essence a family of many thousands and with very strong traditions—will make changes in the agricultural sector a very delicate affair. The influence of traditions or ancient rules of behaviour, and the cultivation of these, are very often fatal in regard to their chance to progress. For centuries or even sometimes millennia priests, sages or chiefs of tribes have aimed at a maintenance of the historic social structure. Some people claim that there is a great inertia in the underdeveloped countries, but it is my firm belief that not inertia, but fear of the sanctions against those disregarding the traditions, is withholding a lot of people from taking an active part in the development of their country.

Although the underdeveloped countries can borrow the most advanced technical methods from the advanced countries, it will not always be possible to introduce them for the reasons we mentioned above. The steady growth of population in the backward countries, and the long time needed to obtain higher yields from the agricultural activities, will very often result in severe difficulties for the governments of the new nations. It will take a long time before hunger is banned for ever!

The next subject to which I shall turn is that of language. In Latin America there are practically no language problems. Each country has the advantage of a single common language—either Spanish, Portuguese, English or French. In Asia a lot of different languages and dialects are used, but for practical reasons English has remained in various countries the language in which official business is carried on. In India, where English is also used in official business, Hindi is spoken by roughly 100 million people, but a lot of other native languages are used too. In Africa the language situation is more

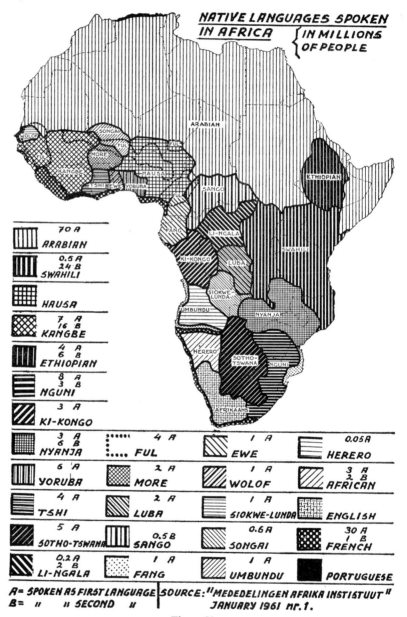

NATIVE LANGUAGES SPOKEN
IN AFRICA {IN MILLIONS
OF PEOPLE

70 A	ARABIAN	
0.5 A / 24 B	SWAHILI	
	HAUSA	
7 A / 16 B	KANGBE	
4 A / 6 B	ETHIOPIAN	
8 A / 3 B	NGUNI	
3 A	KI-KONGO	

3 A / 6 B NYANJA	4 A FUL	1 A EWE	0.05A HERERO
6 A YORUBA	2 A MORE	1 A WOLOF	3 A / 2 B AFRICAN
4 A TSHI	2 A LUBA	1 A SIOKWE-LUNDA	ENGLISH
5 A SOTHO-TSWANA	0.5 B SANGO	0.6A SONGAI	30 A / 1 B FRENCH
0.2 A / 2 B LI-NGALA	1 A FANG	1 A UMBUNDU	PORTUGUESE

A= SPOKEN AS FIRST LANGUAGE
B= "   " SECOND "

SOURCE: "MEDEDELINGEN AFRIKA INSTISTUUT"
JANUARY 1961 nr.1.

Figure V

confusing. There are more than a thousand different languages and
dialects and this results in a lack of philosophical and cultural unity.
In the African countries belonging to the Communauté and in the

70

Commonwealth, respectively, French and English are the official languages as none of the African languages is spoken by enough people to use it as the official language. Figure V gives an impression of the various and most important native African languages. A nation with a single common language possesses a very strong cement of national unity and this can also be said for regions. In Asia and still more in Africa we miss this unifying tool. Without a common language between the peoples of Africa, unification of the whole of Africa will be wishful thinking. It will be understood that the language problem influences seriously the education of the people of the backward nations. Progress in these countries may be held up if not one of the modern European languages is accepted as the official language.

Most people have the idea that the underdeveloped nations are very poor, but in a great many cases they are not! On the contrary, most of the backward countries are rich in material resources and latent human capacities. They are backward because the original population, every bit as good as the colonial power, has very often not developed or even not discovered the available potency. Resource surveys are a prerequisite of economic development which must not be underestimated, but these will only yield results if Western technical assistance is accepted to explore these material resources. Only experienced explorers will be able to produce an exhaustive resource survey and but a few underdeveloped countries will have such experts among their own people.

Until a few years after the last war it was usual to emphasize the poverty of Africa and the general idea was that the chances for economic progress were not very hopeful. Today we know much better. I need only to mention the oil and natural gas in the Sahara, the uranium in Congo, the diamonds and iron ore in Sierra Leone, the copper, gold and diamonds in Tanganyika, the belt of aluminium ore running for 1700 miles from Angola to Guinea, the oilfields of the Niger Delta, and so I could continue this enumeration of the mineral deposits of Africa. Asia and Latin America, too, are rich in material resources. There is a good chance that resource surveys will result in a discovery of raw materials in underdeveloped countries hitherto unacquainted with the hidden richness of their soil.

In consequence of this ignorance of the richness of their own soil, a lot of the underdeveloped countries have concentrated their economic activities on just a few products. Too often the result of such a dependence on the revenues of just one product, making up more than 50% of the total export yield, makes the national economy very vulnerable, especially when the prices on the world market of the

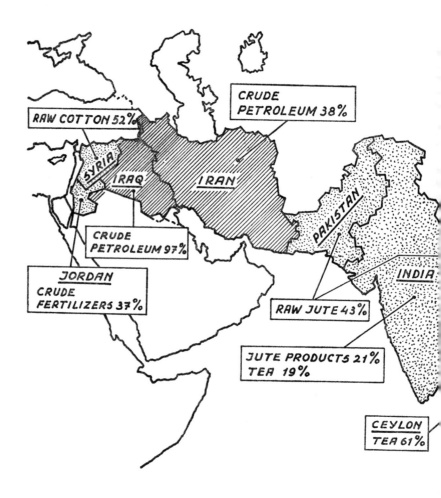

RAW COTTON 52%

CRUDE
PETROLEUM 38%

SYRIA

IRAQ

IRAN

PAKISTAN

CRUDE
PETROLEUM 97%

JORDAN
CRUDE
FERTILIZERS 37%

INDIA

RAW JUTE 43%

JUTE PRODUCTS 21%
TEA 19%

CEYLON
TEA 61%

Source: calculated from:
        Yearbook of international trade-
        statistics 1960 U.N.

Figure VI

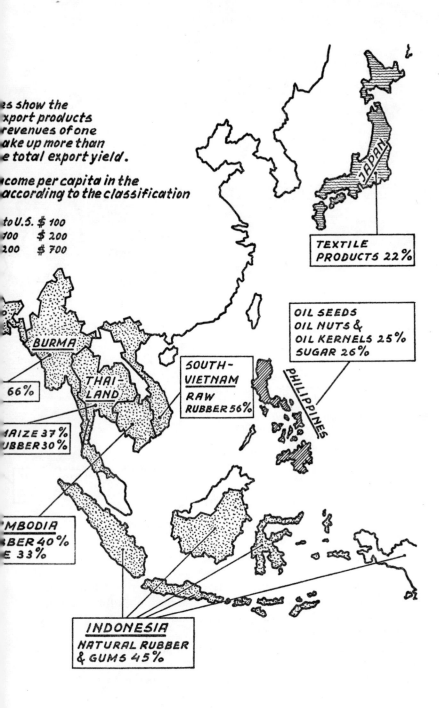

...es show the
...xport products
...revenues of one
...ake up more than
...e total export yield.

...come per capita in the
...according to the classification

...to U.S. $ 100
...100 $ 200
...200 $ 700

TEXTILE
PRODUCTS 22%

OIL SEEDS
OIL NUTS &
OIL KERNELS 25%
SUGAR 26%

BURMA

THAI-
LAND

JAPAN

PHILIPPINES

SOUTH-
VIETNAM
RAW
RUBBER 56%

66%

...AIZE 37%
...UBBER 30%

...MBODIA
...BER 40%
...E 33%

INDONESIA
NATURAL RUBBER
& GUMS 45%

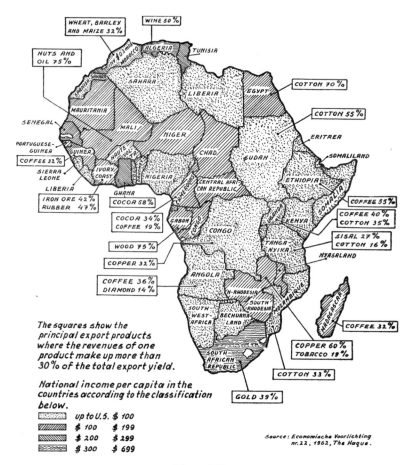

WHEAT, BARLEY AND MAIZE 32%
WINE 50%
NUTS AND OIL 75%
COTTON 70%
COTTON 55%
COFFEE 32%
IRON ORE 42% RUBBER 47%
COCOA 58%
COCOA 34% COFFEE 19%
WOOD 75%
COPPER 32%
COFFEE 36% DIAMOND 14%
COFFEE 55%
COFFEE 40% COTTON 35%
SISAL 27% COTTON 16%
COFFEE 32%
COPPER 60% TOBACCO 19%
COTTON 33%
GOLD 39%

The squares show the principal export products where the revenues of one product make up more than 30% of the total export yield.

National income per capita in the countries according to the classification below.

	up to U.S. $ 100
	$ 100 $ 199
	$ 200 $ 299
	$ 300 $ 699

Source: Economische Voorlichting nr. 22, 1962, The Hague.

Figure VII

product concerned are subject to considerable fluctuations. Diversification of products is a necessity!

The exploration and exploitation of the material resources requires very often a substantial increase in capital investment and for that reason most of the underdeveloped countries will need help from the advanced countries. Funds are needed, both for the project that is immediately revenue-producing and for such basic facilities as roads, railways, port facilities, etc.

It is regrettable that the governments of some underdeveloped or developing countries are following a policy that may hold up their economic progress. An example of such a policy is to be found in Brazil. On the one hand this country welcomes foreign capital, on the other hand it refuses to admit foreign oil companies to explore

74

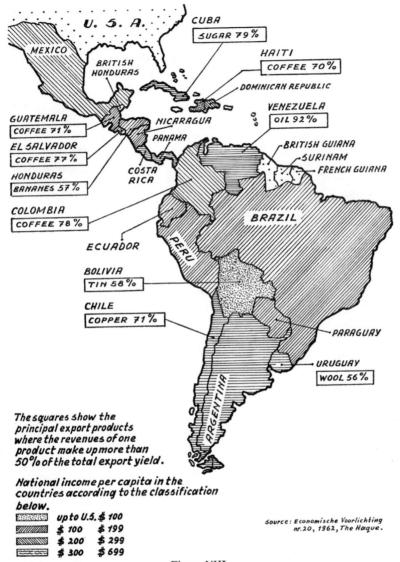

The squares show the principal export products where the revenues of one product make up more than 50% of the total export yield.

National income per capita in the countries according to the classification below.

up to U.S. $ 100	
$ 100	$ 199
$ 200	$ 299
$ 300	$ 699

Source: Economische Voorlichting nr. 20, 1962, The Hague.

Figure VIII

and to exploit the oilfields. Brazil is believed to have very substantial deposits of oil, but so far the State Oilfields Administration (Petrobas) has not had marked success in its prospecting. The result is that the bulk of oil, imported at heavy cost in foreign exchange, has an unfavourable influence on the balance of payments. When we realize this considerable wealth in material resources in the underdeveloped

75

countries and also imagine what it would mean if the Soviets could lay their hands on these resources by bringing the new nations within their sphere of influence, nobody in the West and the free world can deny that such a thing would enormously influence the political and economic balance between East and West, and surely not in our favour. Our strategic position would be weakened and for that reason it is understandable why I pay such attention to the necessity of keeping the new nations outside the Communist sphere of political influence and domination.

As contrasted with the example of Brazil I would like to cite a statement by President Tubman: "We have the natural resources here, but neither the skills nor the money to develop them. Outside private enterprise has the skill and finances to turn our resources into a productivity from which we both benefit. The Unification Program provides a stable, harmonious nation in which private enterprise can flourish, and a flourishing private enterprise gives unity to a nation". Furthermore this intelligent African statesman said: "We Liberians are firm believers in private enterprise as the most efficient and economical way of doing business".[16] As a result of this policy Liberia is now one of the world's biggest suppliers of iron ore. National income, in 1945 scarcely a million dollars, is now 30 times that amount, although large sums have been spent for preliminary work of exploration and development! This example of Liberia shows that the ability of the underdeveloped nations to finance their own development may be rather greater than most people think.

I need not mention the profits gained by the countries of the Middle East as a result of the oil concessions to the Western oil firms, although these revenues are not sufficiently used for economic development and a rise in the standard of living for all. Oil concessions in Libya and the concessions in Tanganyika to explore the diamond fields are other examples of a policy to accelerate economic progress and to raise the national income by foreign private enterprise and investment. Figures VI, VII and VIII give a rough idea of the considerable wealth in natural resources of a number of underdeveloped countries in Asia, Africa and Latin America. If the capital investments for the exploration and exploitation of the material resources are made available to the underdeveloped nations of Asia and Africa, as well as to the developing countries of Latin and Central America, and the governments of nations concerned allow foreign investment, it will accelerate economic progress considerably. Exploitation of the material resources requires, as I pointed out before, all kinds of

16. G. Scullin, A visit with Tubman, President of Liberia, Think, June 1962.

basic facilities. Today the underdeveloped nations badly need "infrastructure", as the modern economic term goes. Roads, waterways, communications, railways, possibly also pipelines, airports, but equally schools and other facilities which are not directly revenue-producing, are the elements of infrastructure. These elements are essential for economic development and have to be available before there can be any thought of revenue-producing economic activities. The rate of development of the "infrastructure" is decisive for the rate of increase in prosperity. Only the advanced countries will be able to provide the new nations with the capital required for the building up of their infrastructure. The faster the infrastructure has been built up, the sooner the economy will reach a point where it is self-propelling and shows a rapid acceleration.

In most of the underdeveloped countries we find only in some areas a more advanced state of development—generally where the former colonists were situated—while in the rest of the country most facilities are lacking. Therefore the development of the various regions to a degree which will permit the gradual reduction of intra-regional disparities is very desirable if not a necessity. However, the foundation of various productive activities in these areas in conjunction with anticipated demographic evolutions will only be logical after the building up of the infrastructure in the whole country. Public investment has to be distributed among the various regions according to their requirements with the purpose of securing the neccessary economic infrastructure.

It will be understood that an order of priorities has to be fixed and also a provisional time-table has to be mapped out. One of the principles that has to be respected in regard to the building up of the infrastructure is that the public utilities programmes and also the public works should correspond with the economic development prospects and that they should suit each individual region. Furthermore, we should not lose sight of the fact that a specific economic activity (mining, plantations, forestry, industry, etc.) ought to correspond with a specific infrastructural outfit. There should not be any non-conformity between the economic activity concerned and the infrastructure.

There is another specific problem I should like to draw attention to. The danger exists that the Communists will in the near future enlarge their influence in the field of economic policy in regard to the underdeveloped countries in another way. The key to extend their influence may not be a larger flow of capital and an increased technical assistance, but a progress in planning methods developed in accordance with the centralized Communist economy. Therefore it is very important to investigate thoroughly how far we in the West have to introduce our new mathematical planning methods in the underdeveloped areas.

When speaking about "new mathematical planning methods" I have in mind in the first place input-output modelling and linear-programming techniques. By using these techniques it is possible to plan the industrial activities, taking into account the inter-industry relations. In the first stages of economic development it is absolutely vital to set up an overall plan of economic growth, giving a full picture of all the interdependences of economic variabilities in aims and means. It is important to realize that the use of the Western decentralized planning methods will preserve the valuable and indispensable place of private enterprise in the economic system of the underdeveloped countries. On the other hand, the Communists with their centralized planning methods want to eliminate any activity in the private sector.

I am deeply convinced that the Western countries have the duty to improve their tools of economic policy used in the aid and technical assistance programmes for the underdeveloped countries, which also means that they should make use of the best qualified and experienced advisers, in order to compete with the Communists in this special topic of "technical assistance" too!

The economic process in most of the underdeveloped nations will show a transformation from pre-industrialization to full-scale industrialization. Although the future will never be forecastable, the infrastructure should always be oriented to the general plans for economic progress, in other wolds the technical composition, the geographical distribution, the size and schedule of realization of the infrastructure have to be subordinated to the superposed industrial activities. In this regard it may be useful to cite Prof. P. M. Rosenstein-Rodan: "Experience of many economic development plans, which are largely pre-industrialization programmes, shows, in fact, that induced industrialization in a non-industrial country or area does not by any means take place automatically. In some cases that may be due to the insufficient size of the social overhead capital investment. In such cases, proceeding with this type of investment until it reaches the minimum quantum of threshold required, it is obviously sensible. In many other cases, however, it does not make sense.

Induced industrialization may not take place for reasons other than those of an insufficient framework of social overhead capital. While the pre-industrialization programme with its large social overhead capital investment is a "conception" of industrialization, the infant industry may not be born without a series of measures of post-natal control".[17] In regard to the question whether priority ought to be given to infrastructure or to industrialization, it is my firm belief that there cannot be talk of a uniform rule. When an underdeveloped country has high-quality mineral resources, an excellent road system and port facilities will be very important in order to obtain the required access to the markets of the advanced countries. However, when considerable funds are spent to extend the network of roads or harbour installations not giving an additional production as a result of this expansion, the investments could have been spent in a better way. Although these projects are of value as a part of the whole programme of development, they may be premature and will sometimes delay other projects giving a higher standard of living sooner. It must be understood that a lot of not immediately revenue-producing facilities, such as education, hospitals, irrigation, communications and similar elements of infrastructure, will always be needed in the first phases of economic development, although they are not sources of prosperity and do not offer employment. The building up of the infrastructure and the measures for pre-industrialization or an improvement of the agricultural system have to go hand in hand, but in such a way that always the highest yield will be obtained. Only in this way will the economies of the underdeveloped countries be brought to a point where they are self-propelling! Too much attention paid to infrastructure and too little but also too late to commercial investments will delay economic progress. All this makes the planning for economic progress of the underdeveloped countries a difficult and complicated affair, which can and may be done only by the most experienced advisers, having a special knowledge of the underdeveloped countries and their populations, but never by theory-mongers somewhere in an advanced country!

Something has to be said about the development programmes. As will be shown when we presently take a closer look at the differences between the various underdeveloped regions and nations, it is impossible to construct a theory on development that can be used everywhere. Also it would be disregarding reality if we were to think that the processes of economic growth will be running parallel in all the underdeveloped countries. The stages of Professor Rostow on the growth to economic maturity have only a theoretical value. The economic growth in Asiatic countries will not be similar to that in African nations or resembles what has taken place in the past in Europe or the United States of America.

Social stratification, religion, education, climate, national re-

17. Prof. P.M. Rosenstein-Rodan. How to industrialize an under-developed area, OEEC publication "Regional Economic Planning", Chapter 9, p. 205.

sources and a lot of other factors will have their specific influence on the lines along which the underdeveloped countries will grow to maturity. It would be wrong if we in our "drive for development", were to try to model the underdeveloped countries upon the structure of the advanced nations of Europe. The "revolution of rising expectations" is forcing the governments of the new nations to an accelerated rate of development and that forces them to a certain dirigism. The Western democratic system of governing is not suitable under these conditions. However, we must not mistake dirigism for dictatorship. Each side in the cold war sincerely believes in the virtuousness of its own political and economic system of society and would like to see the same kind of society established in the underdeveloped countries, but the social stratification of the societies, their level of education, their religion, climatic conditions, landscape, etc. are so different that we cannot use the Western or the Communist system as a general blueprint for the development programme for the new nations.

The size and density of population, the availability of natural resources, the division of labour among different skills, crafts and trades, the climate and the geographic location all have an enormous influence on the lines along which the development may take place. Some of the new nations are relatively small in size or have a population below the figure of one million inhabitants, while others have a substantial size with a variety of soils and climatic conditions for growing a wide range of agricultural products or many material resources. A large size of population will provide the possibility of a large market for agricultural products as well as for consumer goods. The more united the society in the underdeveloped country is, the more inner coherence there exists, the easier it will be for the governments to organize and to work out the plans for economic development. In Congo, where this unity is lacking and only Katanga is showing a certain degree of prosperity, unification is a very difficult affair. All the activities of the United Nations will not lead to very much success as the primary condition—the loyalty and sense of social obligation for a unified Congo is hampered by the existence of different tribes, differences in economic conditions, education, etc. Artificial unification by the use of force will temporarily seem to lead to success, but as soon as the pressure has been lifted, a clash between the opposing groups or tribes will break out afresh.

The history of Europe, where artificial splits of nations or confluences of peoples of different language, religion or historical origin occured, has proved that changes forced upon populations by force or a peace treaty lead in most cases to new calamities. Therefore, we should beware of a too firm drive to unification or the artificial creation of a new society in order to satisfy our intentions to speed up the development of the underdeveloped countries. In this regard we must also realize that the boundaries of a former Western colony do not always imply that the native population of such a colony is a unity, but too often it will be a combination of different and hostile groups or tribes living more or less peacefully together under the force of the colonial power. As soon as independence is obtained, the controversies flare up and threaten the existence of the new nations. I need only mention the problems in India with Kashmir or the guerilla in Indonesia, where peoples of another race or religion are fighting against the supremacy of the Javanese. For this reason the right in self-determination, as laid down in the Charter of the United Nations, has so much sense and has to be respected. Time may weaken the controversies between tribes, races, religious groups and peoples, although that will be time-consuming. Forced and over-hasty unification to speed up economic development, although desirable to accelerate the economic progress and to establish a more diversified and economic unity, may spoil all our efforts to bring prosperity to the population of the underdeveloped world. Time may little by little weaken the existing controversies and economic interests may help to create a better understanding for the necessity of unification or close economic co-operation, whereas artificial unification, by pressure on the side of the United Nations or Western powers, will merely unchain resistance and obstruction.

Our development programmes must reckon with these controversies and all who are concerned with the regional or national economic planning of the underdeveloped areas need a very thorough knowledge of the history, social stratification, composition of population, religion, political situation and other special features of the underdeveloped nations or areas. A journey of some weeks to an underdeveloped nation will never enable an inexperienced adviser, however capable he may be in a specific field, to make a sound appreciation of the local circumstances and to assist in setting up a workable plan for economic development of an underdeveloped nation or region! Amateurishness and the use of inexperienced advisers (although they may just have finished a university education) will cause incalculable harm to the gigantic task the advanced nations have taken on their shoulders in helping the underdeveloped nations to grow to maturity. My criticism may sound unpleasant, but the facts I will present below will, I hope, justify this view.

One of the problems we are meeting is that the leaders of some underdeveloped countries are not satisfied with a sound but time-consuming economic development of their nation, but prefer to concentrate all their efforts and the aid they receive on a few very impressive projects. Just as the Pharaohs of ancient Egypt spent enormous sums of capital and used a considerable labour force to build the pyramids as symbols of greatness and authority, the ambitious leaders of a few new nations have the odd idea that their countries will gain respect and authority in the international political world if their ambassadors abroad are driving in luxurious cars and staying at the most expensive hotels, and if their representatives are taking part in the hundreds of international committees or conferences, or if they establish a huge steelmill (Egypt), a cement factory (Iran) or a national air transport organization (Ethiopia and Ghana). Such a behaviour and such projects do not promote economic development in the fundamental sense of contributing to a self-sustaining growth in the standard of living of the population. Such activities are a drain on the economic resources of the nation, instead of a contribution to their economic strength. The cost of making steel or cement is very much greater than the cost of buying these products elsewhere and therefore these pyramids of modern industry are for the first few decades to come a serious drain on the economic resources of the nations concerned. The money spent by the central governments on these "show business" projects is not only hampering private enterprise but it will also result in a reduction of the funds required for much more important economic activities of general value to the national economic development and progress. Therefore I may conclude that the government of a new nation should not put money in any undertaking or project unless it is sure that it will fit in well with the whole plan for the economic development of the country, but also that the absorbed resources for the project could not be better used in some alternative way. In connexion with this conclusion, it may be worth while to quote Professor P. T. Bauer concerning the economic policy in India: "The massive programme for the establishment of capacity in heavy industry (a capacity not designed to increase the flow of consumer goods for a long time) was a major factor behind the inflationary pressure in recent years in India, which in turn was largely responsible for the unplanned exchange crisis. This crisis issued in sudden discontinuous changes in policy, including the suspension of public and private projects and the imposition and extension of controls over the allocation of resources, including imports, materials and components. Such measures inhibit effective longterm planning in both the public and the private sectors, and they also inflate costs, thus obstructing both the growth of resources and their most

82

effective allocation. Moreover, the determination to proceed with this programme at all costs has necessitated severe restrictions on the import and even on the local production of consumer goods, including the virtual elimination of certain important categories. This result of the emphasis on heavy industry implies obvious hardship. Moreover, such measures necessarily affect entire categories of commodities and they cannot be adjusted to allow for the circumstances and conditions of particular areas, enterprises and individuals, which aggravates the waste".[18]

We know that today India is still seriously handicapped by those wretched ambitions in regard to heavy industry and is now facing difficulties in meeting the requirements of the present plans for development. The price it has to pay in the form of a retardation of economic progress for over-ambitious projects is really very high and regrettable.

However impressive it may be to show visiting foreigners a huge steelmill or an electric power station, economic history has shown that also without these "pyramids of modern industrialization" economic progress and growth to maturity may be obtained. A lot of predominantly agricultural countries of Europe have grown to the stage of high mass-consumption without the burden of a concentration of their economic activities on heavy industry. Japan is another example of a development to maturity with a less ambitious planning for economic progress.

The big mistake made by many of the leaders of the new nations is that they want to bring about a transformation in their societies in the shortest time, forgetting that it took the advanced countries a whole century and more to reach their present level of prosperity. The dynamic progress of science and technology in the advanced countries has enlarged the world's problems out of all proportion to the past and the growing gap between the West and the underdeveloped countries can only be narrowed by sound and harmonious economic planning of the development of the underdeveloped world, but not by the creation of just a few impressive symbols of national prestige or "pyramids of modern technology" in an, all along the line, underdeveloped society. Although the advanced countries are able to speed up the economic progress in the underdeveloped world and especially when the new nations are willing to make full use of the experience and the new methods of economic planning, so that they need not follow the same time-consuming traditional ways of the economic growth to maturity of ancient Europe, it

18. Prof. P. T. Bauer, Indian Economic Policy and Development, London, 1961, p. 55.

is impossible to fill the gap in development between the West and the underdeveloped world in a couple of years. This will take decades!

Professor M. Friedman has arrived at a conclusion that all these "modern monuments" contrasting with the real stage of economic development of the rest of the underdeveloped country are introducing rigidity and inflexibility and therefore he objects to a centralized programme of economic development. In his view such centralized programmes, with their state enterprises are a threat to the preservation of a free world and will speed up communization in underdeveloped countries.[19] When we take a look at a number of government enterprises in more or less underdeveloped countries, we see very often an enormous waste of capital. Also we see that a lot of opportunities are not used to the full extent. A good example is given by Professor R. de O. Campos. He wrote in connexion with Brazil: "The north-eastern area (of Brazil), although comprising one-fourth of the population of the country, accounts for only 11 per cent of the national income. The investments of the federal government in the area have been increasing in recent years, but due to lack of co-ordination and inadequate planning these have not been very effective. For instance, substantial investments in water reservoirs as a protection against droughts had been made in the last two decades without the complementary irrigation works. Thus, while the accumulated water could theoretically irrigate 160,000 hectares, only 5,000 were actually irrigated in 1959".[20]

I have mentioned already the production of steel and cement, respectively in Egypt and near Abadan, at prices much higher than would have to be paid for imports of these products. Too little attention has been given to the question whether these projects will be profitable or not. When the central government and other public authorities occupy themselves with projects not belonging to the field of public utilities or infrastructure, far too much control is placed in their hands and that will restrict but also hamper private enterprise. Where capital is scarce in underdeveloped countries, too much investment by the governments in projects for which private capital could be obtained will result in a retardation in infrastructural projects. Also we see too often that a lot of governmental projects are started too light-heartedly. In this regard I would like to give an example of an over-ambitious project in Venezuela. When I say here

19. Prof. M. Friedman, Foreign Economic Aid: Means and Objectives, Yale Review, June 1958.
20. Prof. R. de O. Campos, Article entitled "Case studies of employment problems and policies", in Employment objectives in economic development, I.L.O., Geneva, 1961, p. 150.

84

"over-ambitious", it has to be seen in the light of the present state of economic development of that nation, when a lot of money is still needed for undertakings giving a more direct and higher yield for the whole national economy. In the case of Venezuela it may be instructive to describe what has happened with the "Siderúrgìca" steel and iron works at Matanza till the moment production started on July 9, 1962. Venezuela is still importing potatoes, pulse, oil-bearing seeds, rice, corn and so on, but after really very small investments, in order to improve the irrigation, Venezuela could have met the home consumption of these products, favouring the balance of payments and also the employment situation. This country has large resources of iron ore of high quality and estimates give the figure of three thousand million tons. United States Steel Corporation and Bethlehem Steel Company were exploiting these resources, giving the following production and export figures:

	production 1000 tons	export 1000 tons	million $	percentage of the total exports of Venezuela
1957	15,296	15,587	116,4	about 5 %
1958	15,485	15,616	117,9	„ 5 %
1959	17,201	17,000	127,8	„ 5.4%
1960	19,490	19,323	167,1	„ 6.6%
1961	14,567	15,029	137,4	„ 6.2%

During the period 1952-1958 plans were made to turn out iron and steel for home consumption and for export. Venezuela is importing per year iron and steel, as well as iron and steel products, to a value of about $ 450 million. The construction of the iron and steel factory "Siderúrgìca", on the border of the Orinoco river, at a distance of 275 kilometres from the sea, started in 1957. An Italian firm partially financed the installation and contracted in 1959 a loan of $ 32,852,000 and a second loan of $ 20,000,000 in 1961. Where possible, equipment made in Italy, Germany, Norway and the U.S.A. was used. Research and future investment will amount $ 363 million, of which 72% has now been paid by the government of Venezuela. The required electric power station with a capacity of 370,000 kw has also been paid as to 70%. Total production of iron and steel as well as iron and steel products will amount 600,000 tons and may be doubled in a following period. This all sounds well and the peak demand will not show any trouble. However, the c.i.f. price of imported steel will be lower and therefore the government of Venezuela is already taking action to prevent imports from the U.S.A. It will be very difficult with regard to the price of the iron and steel products of Venezuela to compete on the world market. This now state-owned project is hampering seriously the development of the coun-

85

try as there has been concentrated too much on one single project. In the long run and especially when Venezuela gets its chance in a Latin American common market, this project may be of high value. However, in my opinion foreign private investment for this project would have been much better, leaving more money available for the numerous and important development projects. It is questionable whether the export of iron ore alone would not have been more profitable, taking into account the existing competition on the world market and the lower prices of other countries manufacturing iron and steel products. If "Siderúrgica" is completely dependent on the home demand as a result of the higher price than elsewhere, it may lead to a financial catastrophe. The experience is that very often also the efficiency in state-owned undertakings leaves much to be desired. I have paid a lot of attention to this example in order to show that over-ambitious and state-owned projects, requiring an enormous investment, are not advisable. Venezuela and India both now have very serious balance of payments problems, but are also retarding their development plans. The oil companies in Venezuela are responsible for 90% of the foreign currency earnings of the country and 40% of the earnings of the government comes from the foreign oil companies. However, the government of Venezuela is now again investing tens of million dollars in a state-owned oil company and it is only the beginning of such an activity. The private oil companies paid their Venezuelan employees very well and offered them outstanding social conditions. The behaviour of the government of Venezuela will discourage private investment in the country and that means a decrease of the inflow of capital, resulting in an unavoidable still more critical balance of payments problem and then the time will come that the advanced countries are asked to help Venezuela with much aid.

Professor Benham wrote in regard to waste of financial aid given by the advanced nations that this must not be an argument for giving no aid at all, but he gave a warning: "They are arguments for making sure that projects are carefully planned; that some are not left incomplete (for example power stations without transmission lines or dams without irrigation canals) for lack of funds; that plant and equipment are suitable for the country and trained workers are available to use them, and that their products can be marketed; that experts are not provided without the necessary equipment or, conversely, that there is co-ordination of aid provided from different sources.[21]

21. F. Benham, Economic aid to underdeveloped countries, London, 1961, p. 102.

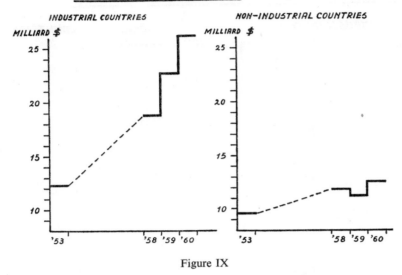

DEMAND FOR INDUSTRIAL PRODUCTS

Figure IX

Technological progress, political changes, increased aid and technical assistance are bringing forward the necessity that development plans are flexible. These plans ought to be subject to revision from time to time, owing to changes as mentioned above. A great deal of thought and thorough investigation will be needed. Always the limitation of resources will force the planners to decide on priorities. Never should resources be absorbed for a certain project when they could be used better in some alternative way!

Nobody will deny that economic progress is a matter of improving the variety and quantity of production, but also asks for an improvement of efficiency. That is the big problem of the underdeveloped nations as they are too often lacking the experienced and well-trained cadre and the development plans or programmes must always take that into account. It is unfortunate that such a lot of errors have been made in the past in regard to the development plans and very often the representatives of the advanced nations and still more those of some multilateral institutions have given a wrong advice, mostly due to inexperience with the specific circumstances in underdeveloped areas.

The governments of the underdeveloped countries have to realize that capital is scarce, although enormous amounts of aid have been given by the advanced countries, and therefore they must be careful to spend no money or anyhow not too much of the national income on just a few projects.

87

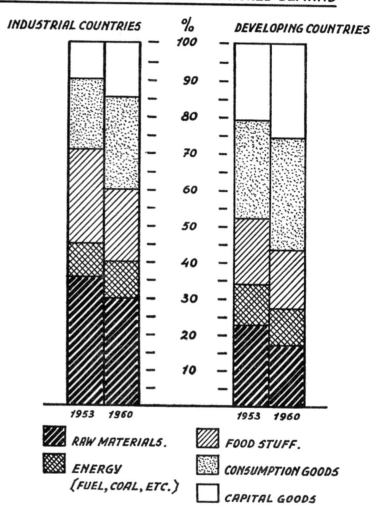

PROPORTIONALLY COMPOSITION OF THE WORLD DEMAND

INDUSTRIAL COUNTRIES

%

DEVELOPING COUNTRIES

1953 1960

1953 1960

RAW MATERIALS.

FOOD STUFF.

ENERGY
(FUEL, COAL, ETC.)

CONSUMPTION GOODS

CAPITAL GOODS

Source: Economische Voorlichting
nr. 11 - 1962.

Figure X

It is really regrettable that we see too much lack of co-ordination
and inadequate planning in regard to the underdeveloped world. I
have mentioned already the fact that too often resource surveys are
lacking or not worked out to the full extent, resulting in a crippled
programme for economic development and delaying economic progress

88

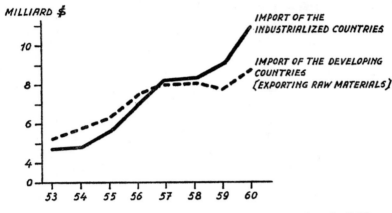

DEMAND FOR CAPITAL GOODS

MILLIARD $

IMPORT OF THE
INDUSTRIALIZED COUNTRIES

IMPORT OF THE DEVELOPING
COUNTRIES
(EXPORTING RAW MATERIALS)

Source: Economische Voorlichting
nr. 14 - 1962.

Figure XI

Too little attention has been paid to the increasing integration of
the economies of all the nations of our world. A look at Figures
VI, VII and VIII shows the dependence of the economies of some
countries on just a few products, but also that some of the underdeveloped nations are competing with each other with the same agricultural
product on the market. In view of our complicated and integrated world economy, but also to promote the trade between
the underdeveloped countries themselves in order to facilitate the
creation of a kind of common market, it is necessary to attune the
national development programmes to each other. Instead of national
development plans we have to achieve area-planning, and at the
same time it must be studied how far these area-development plans
are well attuned to the whole economy. In Figure IX we see the
difference in the demand for industrial products in the industrial
and the non-industrial countries in the period from 1953 till 1960.
It means for the time being a growing gap between the economies
of the advanced and the underdeveloped world. It will be very difficult for the developing economies, with a lack of technological
knowledge, experience and a skilled labour force, to compete on the
markets of the advanced countries with their industrial products.
This will only be possible with products where the labour cost plays
an important role in the cost price. Japan, with its lower labour cost, was
for that reason able to conquer a considerable place on the Western

89

markets. Of course some underdeveloped countries will have a chance with some specific national products or products which those countries are able to produce under very favourable conditions. Gabon, a small African country of 400,000 inhabitants having at its disposal Okoumé, an excellent kind of wood, is able to export three-ply wood and railway sleepers at competitive prices. It is my firm belief that it is possible, by paying full attention to the planning and promotion of trade between the underdeveloped countries within certain areas, to help to accelerate the economic progress and to establish there a footing for a common market, especially for not too complicated products and certain consumer goods, whilst attention is to be paid to a diversification in the production of the manufactured goods in the various partners in that area. This will be all the more necessary as the advanced countries are using relatively more and more artificial raw materials and as a result of that the demand for raw materials from the underdeveloped nations is decreasing. It is understandable that a large quantity of essential raw materials will always have to be bought in the underdeveloped world as there are no substitutes for them. Figure X gives an idea of the procentual demand in the industrial and non-industrial countries. It shows the considerable decrease of demand by the advanced countries for raw materials and foodstuffs, which are especially the products exported by the underdeveloped nations. The export of food and allied products—going for 73% to the industrialized countries—showed a decrease from 23% in 1953 to 18% in 1960. We may draw the conclusion from this Figure that procentually the demand for products from the underdeveloped world is decreasing, but that on the other hand especially the demand for capital goods of the advanced countries is increasing. We need not explain the influence of this tendency on the balance of payments of the under-developed countries. Figure XI shows the import of capital goods in the industrial countries and the underdeveloped raw materials producing countries. The disappointing conclusion we draw from Figures IX and X is that there is a tendency towards a growing gap between the exports and imports in the underdeveloped countries. Aid from the advanced countries has helped them partly out of their balance of payments problem. It is my firm belief that only a well diversified industrialization programme, especially giving priority to medium-size industries, making use of the specific resources of each nation, may help to narrow the gap. Industrial activities, asking for too high capital investments, are for some time not to be recommended. Therefore private investment will be of the highest importance to speed up industrialization in order to make the countries

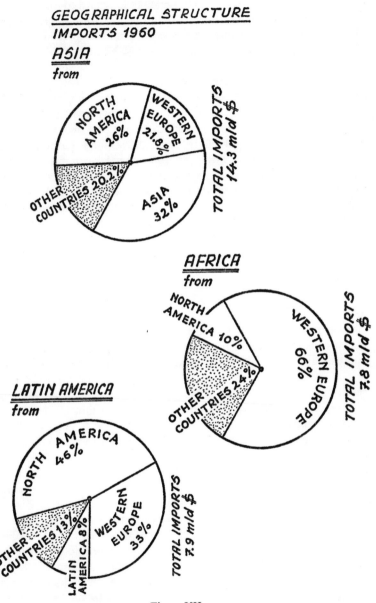

GEOGRAPHICAL STRUCTURE
IMPORTS 1960

ASIA
from

NORTH AMERICA 26%
WESTERN EUROPE 21.8%
OTHER COUNTRIES 20.2%
ASIA 32%
TOTAL IMPORTS 14.3 m/d $

AFRICA
from

NORTH AMERICA 10%
WESTERN EUROPE 66%
OTHER COUNTRIES 24%
TOTAL IMPORTS 7.8 m/d $

LATIN AMERICA
from

NORTH AMERICA 46%
OTHER COUNTRIES 13%
LATIN AMERICA 8%
WESTERN EUROPE 33%
TOTAL IMPORTS 7.9 m/d $

Figure XII

less dependent on their exports of raw materials and their tropical
or subtropical agricultural products.

It is becoming increasingly recognized that planning has many dimensions and in this case it is not enough in regard to the economic development programme to pay attention only to a single new nation. Planning for a whole area is needed and even then it has to be well attuned to the whole world economy. Neglect of this necessity will be disastrous!

Furthermore it may be worthwhile for the advanced countries to realize the consequences of this state of affairs with, regard to the balance of payments problem of the underdeveloped countries, as their trade with them will be affected. Figure XII shows the procentual import pattern in 1960 in Asia, Africa and Latin America. This Figure also shows how important the African market is for Europe, while both North America and Western Europe account for the largest part of the imports in Latin America. Recently Western Europe has been increasing its exports to Latin America at the expense of the United States. This Figure also proves the importance of the markets in the underdeveloped world for the Western economies. Therefore, there is every reason to pay full attention to the aid programmes and to technical assistance for the underdeveloped world, but no less to the necessity to send the best and most experienced advisers for the difficult task of drawing up the development programmes.

Finally I would like to give a well-meant warning to those countries having a clear preference for state-owned enterprises. All the developing countries are in need of capital and the nations welcoming private investment may then see an increased inflow of capital, resulting in an accelerated development but also in a considerable increase of employment. The latter is very important in view of the growth of population. Also more chances to find a suitable job are becoming available for their college-taught élite. Furthermore, when private investment is hampered in the developing countries that capital may be used for new undertakings in the advanced countries and instead of narrowing the gap in development and prosperity between the advanced countries and the developing world, this will be enlarged. The psychological effect in the advanced countries might be in the future, if the governments of certain developing countries are hindering private investment or promoting over-ambitious state-owned enterprises, that pressure is put on the governments of the advanced countries to decrease or perhaps even to stop aid in any form to developing countries with such an attitude!

CHAPTER V

TECHNICAL ASSISTANCE

The complex process by which an underdeveloped country moves ahead to maturity is by no means always thoroughly understood. Economic enrichment and social progress have become world-wide and the touchstone of maturity and modernity for all nations, advanced or underdeveloped. Out of the discussion of means to these desired ends has come a new conception of education as the principal vehicle of social and economic progress. There is pressure in all parts of the world today to expand public education. Education is now recognized as one of the forces, if not the principal one, behind economic growth. The smaller the number of skilled and educated people, the more difficult it is to develop a society to a higher level of economic growth. However, education is a very time-consuming affair, but on the other hand the new nations are anxious to grow in the shortest time to economic maturity. They have obtained independence, but now they come to realize that they are in need of the experienced people to perform the innumerable functions in the government, public services and private undertakings. In order to speed up the required development the developing countries are forced to make use of foreign human resources. They need the help of experienced people and the advanced countries only are able and willing to place them at the disposal of the underdeveloped nations till these countries are able to run their own affairs. However, technical assistance is not and must never be an effort to obtain political influence and the Western countries have never left the developing nations in doubt about this!

Technical assistance offered to developing countries by international institutions, by governments or private institutions and firms, has expanded considerably in recent years. Coordination between economic aid as well as private enterprise and technical assistance will greatly increase the effectiveness of the flow of Western funds to the underdeveloped countries. Assistance should be rendered to developing countries for assessing their employment problems and formulating economic plans which take full account of these problems.

In this chapter I will be dealing with the investment in human resources and the various aspects of this enormous task.

"Technical assistance" or "technical aid" is a phrase which is often used, but too many people do not know clearly what it involves. Even international and national organizations or institutes which give such help find it hard to agree on what it means. Although there is in official circles no need for an exact definition, for my purpose it is desirable to give a general description of the activities which are covered under the expression "technical assistance" in order to enable me to comment on the various aspects. In my opinion it covers the education of the people of the developing countries in the broadest sense, the building up of their institutions and services, giving advice with regard to the raising of their standards of living, including the social aspect thereof, and finally giving advice with regard to the development of their natural resources and their planning for economic progress.

The former colonial powers have too often given inadequate attention to investment in education and technical training. We may partly impute this to a policy intended to prevent too strong a drive for independence by the native population in the pre-war days, but also to a certain lethargy of the latter.

In the backward nations there was a great inertia, very often influenced by the traditional structure of the society. Aujoulat describes how an old chief of an African tribe complained of the fact that the white men sent in turn to him as advisers has deprived him of his authority and the chiefs of the tribes were no longer entitled to give orders, and their judgments too were no longer respected. Young Africans who had finished primary school told him that they were very disappointed as a result of the fact that they were not allowed by the elder people of the tribe to do more than work in the field and carry heavy loads on their head to the market, just as they did before going to school. They asked: "Now then, what is the sense of going to school?"[22] At the moment we are still meeting such passive obstruction within certain groups against all the undertakings to raise the level of education although the new governments are promoting and supporting all educational activities by all means.

Acces to education is increasingly regarded not only as a "human right" but also as a basic condition for economic growth. In any democratic or non-Communist society the right to education is now generally recognized without any restriction with regard to the existing political system, but the conviction that education will only have a practical effect in developing countries if it keeps pace with the economic development of the society is now also widespread. Discrimination must be wiped out and education has to be made

22. L. P. Aujoulat, Aujourd'hui l'Afrique, Paris 1960, p. 106 and p. 116.

available to everyone who is especially talented. In modern times (and that applies in particular to the developing countries) we cannot afford to spoil any part of the human resources and skills. Economic progress not only depends on the input of capital per head of the population, but also to a large extent on the abilities and the character of the population, especially on its willingness to learn and to apply improved methods of production, administration and organization, but also on the skill, qualities and education of its own entrepreneurs. The greatest significance of a new approach based upon an intensive aid programme lies in the battle for men's minds in the developing countries and it will be the rise of the general level of education that will promote a better understanding of the intentions of the advanced countries in connexion with their aid programmes. The young independent nations will have to understand that their economic development is an affair of reciprocal interest—both for themselves and for the advanced countries — in order to stabilize and to improve the political and economic relations in the free world.

The two main objects of the educational policy, within general national policy, are to meet the demands of individuals for their own well-being and to meet the needs of society for its general development.

The result of the rapid technological progress and the increasing intricacy of the present economic system have placed a premium on education and particularly on the flexibility of mind. Therefore, the task of educating everybody, within the limits of his mental gifts, is of vital importance for an effective way of living in a complicated and continuously changing environment. In the developing countries a huge rise in the level of education is the only way to alleviate the existing poverty and backwardness. A policy for education cannot be based on present conditions, because its social, economic and technological result will be felt over a long period in the future. On the other hand we have to take care that we are not overhasty in this field, by which we could do more harm than good to the developing country. It is not sensible to try to invest on a large scale in a country until the preliminary work of training its basic skilled manpower and cadres has been done, but on the other hand we must also take care that the future demand for people with a high-school or college education is not too ambitious, in order to avoid a situation where suitable jobs would not be available for them. The latter would give rise, for example, to a surplus in the category of lawyers or economists and a shortage of engineers or physicians.

Today, one of the most serious problems in the developing countries is that a considerable number of middle-class and higher employments are lacking. It will result in tension and dissatisfaction if a number of students of the underdeveloped nations are re-entering their own country while the latter cannot offer them suitable jobs in the organization of the government or in private enterprise.

Poverty is a primary reason for the inability in some of the new nations to support a substantial middle-class and the result of that is the lack of jobs for college-taught youngsters. Foreign private investment and activities could help to create suitable jobs for a considerable number of the young élite of the new nation.

It is understandable that there is an immense need for training of all kinds, from on-the-job training of artisans to the more complex sciences, but the education planning has to be attuned to the development of the whole society within a certain calculable period. I would like to warn against the problems that will be created if the new governments in their drive for rapid industrialization, promote the flow to the towns of non- or half-educated youngsters from the backward regions with still primitive living conditions and a traditional social structure.

Remodelling education of the youngsters to develop skill in farming and to modernize agricultural methods must preferably be done in the rural regions and that implies the foundation of schools for agricultural instruction in these regions.

The usual experience is that the new nations are not lacking the operative at the bench, but the people trained for the middle ranges of industrial activities, and that means at the level of foreman and factory manager. The foundation of primary and secondary technical schools must get high priority.

It is my firm belief that it is preferable to establish the universities, high schools, technical schools and so forth in the developing countries themselves. First of all, I consider it an enormous gain if the instructors, partly made available by the advanced countries within the framework of their technical assistance programmes, are able to make themselves familiar with the specific local problems for the benefit of their instruction; secondly, the pupils are staying in their own atmosphere with the familiar living conditions, while the costs of the education for the government can be kept low.

The pupils sent for their education to the cities—like the migrants going to work in the industries—are perhaps very cruelly treated as they are not familiar with the often dynamic transformation going on in the underdeveloped countries. Away from the familiar atmosphere of the native village and plunged into the insecure and bewildering life in town, requiring a completely new set of attitudes towards life, behaviour and work, they will feel themselves more or less lost. The gap between the traditional way of living in the old rural village and the restless hard life of the city may throw a lot of the pupils out of their balance, influencing the results of their studies. By analogy I think that it will be much better to establish universities in the developing countries instead of sending the aspiring students to those in the advanced nations. Besides this, the students will not get a feeling of superiority over their countrymen, based on the fact that they have travelled around a large part of the world. Furthermore, these students do not get used to a way of living which they will not meet for decades in their own country. There is a serious cause for alarm when we see how many students of developing nations prefer to settle down for ever in the Western towns where they finished their studies—Paris, London, Rome, New York and so forth. These youngsters have got familiar with all the luxury of the Western way of living. They meet girls and sometimes marry them, but most of these girls will not be very eager to settle down in an underdeveloped country and the man who could be of such value to his own nation is lost for ever. People may say that we need not take this too seriously, but one would really be surprised to know the number of coloured students who do not return to their own country. Too many coloured students after their college days, prefer the easier life in a Western town to a hard job in a backward region in their own country as an engineer or a surgeon. One will experience the drawback of an education at a European or American university, getting back uprooted Africans or Asiatics who could not find a suitable job or could not accustom themselves to the primitive life in their own country.

Branislaw Malinowski already wrote in 1943 about the problems of the African youngsters and therefore it may be of some use to cite what has been written in the summary preceding his article: "The young African today lives in two worlds and belongs fully to neither. European education has alienated him from native traditions and imbues him with the values and expectations of European culture. At the same time European interests exclude him from the white community and deny him the material basis for the style of life he has been taught to aspire to. Education must be transformed to close rather than perpetuate the gap between expectations and reality. African schools should train their pupils for adaptation to the African environment. Respect for native values should be maintained along with the equipment for co-operation with the European community. European wealth should be used to provide the basis for fulfilling the claims and needs which Western education has developed.[23] Too often

23. Branislaw Malinowski: The Pan-African problem of culture contact; American Journal of Sociology, XLVIII, 6, 1943, p. 649.

the coloured students have themselves chosen, or have been advised to choose, a course of study at the university which for the present is of little value for the development of their country or does not give them an income large enough to live on, resulting in a return to the advanced country where they finished their studies.

The country may need more engineers, surgeons or economists than artists, but more of its young people may wish to specialize in art, biology or modern languages than prepare themselves for one of the other jobs mentioned. However this conflict between the choice of the individual and national policy-making may be more apparent than real. Individuals in general cannot be expected to be perfectly informed about the chance to make subsequent full use of their study and to earn enough to live on, but also the preference for a certain course of study is too often based on very vague ideas and impressions. Vocational guidance forms the best and most important link between the national policy and the choice of the individual. On the other hand, restrictions on the free choice of the course of study have to be accepted so long as public funds for education and the possibilities of receiving an education are inadequate in relation to demand. This means for the time being that students' preferences cannot generally be met. It may be that the youngster feels this restriction as a discrimination and for that reason it may be preferable to leave the decision on this matter to his own government, familiar with the existing needs in accordance with the future development.

In a democracy belonging to the so-called advanced countries, the individual is free in the choice of the subject of his study and fundamentally this should be the same for the youngsters in an underdeveloped country. However, the need to have at the disposal of the new nations the required élite (intellectuals skilled in different areas of science) and the fact that the costs of study are usually paid by an advanced country or a multilateral organization, may justify for the present a system whereby the course of study anticipates the requirements of the developing nation. Not only will the future of the student in his native country be secured but also the money of the bilateral or multilateral funds for technical assistance would be spent in the most profitable way.

Irrespective of the preceding remarks, I am strongly convinced that it might be preferable to establish universities in the developing countries instead of sending the coloured students to Europe or America. I realize that it will be difficult to get the best teachers willing to work for some time in an underdeveloped country. However, salaries can be made very attractive. The quality of the Western teachers at a university in the developing world may gain enormously as these teachers are able to get more familiar with the specific situation and conditions of the nation where they are educating their students. They will notice that what theoretically is the best solution of a problem cannot always be used in an underdeveloped country. A lot of coloured students, returning after their studies at a university in Europe or America, will be very disappointed when they come to realize that what has been taught by theory-mongers at Western universities—unfamiliar with the situation in underdeveloped societies—is only fitting in an advanced country. These students will get confused and may get a feeling that they are being misled.

Nevertheless it may be advisable to offer a chance to some of the most talented coloured students to go to one of the Western universities and thus to get a better understanding of the advanced world, so that afterwards they will be able to realize the differences in development and way of living in the West and the new nation. However, this is not a necessity for all.

I think that the people in the developing countries will have more appreciation for someone who comes to teach them at their university and sacrifices himself to such a heavy task, than for the theory-mongers somewhere in an advanced country. In our Western scientific circles there is too little knowledge of the real conditions in the underdeveloped countries, and by knowledge I mean the combination of theory and experience.

Now I will pass to another aspect of technical assistance. Education is, as I mentioned above, a time-consuming affair and will bear fruit after many years only, but the governments of the new nations need advice right now because they lack an élite large enough and fit for the complicated job of developing a nation to economic maturity. We in the West, who had to find our way by trial and error, are able to speed up the development of the new nations with our experience by giving technical advice. However, there is a large difference between the circumstances as they are in the Western countries and those in subtropical or tropical areas with a population consisting to a large extent of illiterate persons, having an archaic social structure, lacking an adequate infrastructure, with primitive health conditions, to say nothing of a lot of traditions hampering a change in the state of affairs. It will be understood that those who have to assist and to advice the governments of the new nations need experience obtained in parts of the world with more or less similar conditions. A young Dutchman, who had just finished his studies in economics and got his master's degree in 1962, was sent a few months later by the United Nations to Egypt to give technical assistance for the next five years. This is not at all an exceptional case! It is not surprising that such an adviser will do more harm than good to the efforts of the West to accelerate the development of the new nations.

The former colonial powers have at their disposal a very large number of people who have gained a lot of experience in official or private jobs in the former colonies. It is understandable that in certain cases the new nations will not appreciate being advised by someone from the country that ruled for a century or longer over its territory and especially not when independence has been obtained after a long period of fighting. However, someone of another nationality, but above all with a large experience in underdeveloped territories with more or less similar conditions, may be an adviser of high value and will be acceptable. He has learned to live under primitive conditions and knows how difficult it is to introduce new systems and methods. He will know how to break through the barriers of tradition of an archaic society and to introduce new ideas and methods, without frustrating the tribe and his chief or the rural society as a whole. He will realize that he will never get to know the people he has to advice if he isolates himself, like sometimes other advisers have done, by spending his evening in his own club—air-conditioned, equipped with refrigerators and all other conveniences making life easy and comfortable. If he wants to be succesful as an adviser he has to renounce a lot of these conveniences and then he will gain confidence. Also he has to be a diplomat in the sense that he does not hurt the sentiments of the native population. Another very important thing is that the advisers are not colour-conscious and in my opinion the prestige and the goodwill of the adviser is also dependent on how far racial discrimination still exists in his own country. White and black labourers are seen working in the same gang, sometimes under a coloured foreman, in the Portuguese colony of Angola and they will be seen as mixed parties in cafés and restaurants. Advisers belonging to former colonial powers where inter-marriage between the colonists and the natives took place and will accordingly have the right attitude towards coloured people, and will be able to prevent a lot of bad feelings and misunderstanding.

It is in the interest of the West that people selected for the difficult and delicate task of advising the developing nations should be able to use their special knowledge and their experience of overseas social and economic problems, but it is a necessity as well that the people in the advanced countries dealing with aid and technical assistance should continuously acquire fresh knowledge about the new nations. I have no objection to using our young college-taught people for technical assistance programmes, but before they are allowed to work on their own, they should first have assisted a well-experienced adviser for a couple of years in an underdeveloped country. It may be worthwhile to refer in this respect to an article in the Moroccan journal Al Itiqlal of March 12, 1960, on page 6 under the significant title: "Expertisons . . . les experts". The author criticizes the flow of United Nations experts to Morocco as a plague of grasshoppers, having a standard far below average and a low morality. But above all they are not at all suitable for the job they have to do. They have got the impression in Morocco that they are saddled sometimes with higher ranking civil servants from an advanced country, who want to escape from their dull offices or try to obtain more "authority as an expert in matters of development of backward countries" or with someone who has to be promoted away through lack of ability.

Billerbeck criticizes in the same way the technical assistance activities of the United Nations. He points to the fact that many advisers are not suitable in their function of adviser. Furthermore, he is of the opinion that there is not very much point in sending a United Nations expert for only six months or at the utmost for a year to a developing country. Their advice will not be worked out thoroughly and also they are brooding with regard to their next appointment and future.[24] Another complaint in the article mentioned above is that the high salaries and the way of living of the foreign experts are rousing jealousy and anger. What is the value of a group of eight experts of the United Nations who managed to establish a small co-operative workshop and taught a group of young woman how to knit. The results of this "succesful" activity were reported, together with percentages and photograps, in international official magazines as an example of the technical assistance successes in Morocco. I will not cite all the complaints as they are presented in this article, however instructive they may be. Fortunately, many examples can also be given of very successful technical assistance, but the article is useful since it supports my idea that a better selection of the advisers from the international organizations for technical assistance is necessary. With such an activity as described in Al Itiqlal we are spoiling our own cause and we will lose goodwill as well as respect, thereby giving the new nations the impression that we do not always take our duties as seriously as required. We may appreciate the feelings of humanity of all those who have made themselves available to the developing nations, but there is more the new nations need than humanity and that is advice based on long-term experience and sound knowledge.

In his address to the Board of Governors of the World Bank on September 18, 1962, Mr. E. R. Black said that the new Development Advisory Service had come into operation. A small corps of highly

24. K. Billerbeck, Reform der Entwicklungshilfe (Auf der Basis bisheriger Erfahrungen), Hamburg 1961, p. 74.

experienced professionals had been recruited to assist the member governments of less developed countries to take up urgent development tasks. They are available to serve as economic and financial advisers, particularly in the preparation and execution of economic development programmes. Some of them were already serving abroad—in Chile, Ghana, Pakistan and Thailand. In the past a vast legion of specialists has gone out from the United Kingdom to every corner of the world, helped forward the people of other countries, and made it possible to develop the natural resources of their lands. These specialists were busy in the field of engineering, surveying, industrial development, mining, tropical agriculture, oil industry and management. For example India, Pakistan and other former British colonies now have an "élite", although still too small for the actual demand of these quickly developing societies. The present-day contribution of the United Kingdom is still very impressive. More than 150,000 Britons have settled in overseas countries, a large part of them going to Commonwealth countries. The United Kingdom is participating also in technical assistance programmes and supplies hundreds of experts to overseas countries and receives thousands of trainees and students for training in Great Britain. The U.K. Government is playing an important part in arranging and financing this flow of experts and trainees through its participation in the Technical Co-operation Scheme of the Colombo Plan, in the Expanded Programme of Technical Assistance (E.P.T.A.) of the United Nations, and a number of other international technical assistance programmes, and by arrangements with the governments of United Kingdom dependencies.

France also has an extremely large number of well-trained and experienced people, willing and able to be used and already working for decades within the former French colonies, but also in other underdeveloped countries. The same can be said for a number of other European countries such as Germany, Italy, Belgium, the Netherlands, and so on. Experience shows that there are certain types of technical assistance which one country is well fitted to supply and another not. For example not all European countries are familiar with tropical agriculture. We have to organize the advanced countries' capacity to meet the demands for technical assistance from the underdeveloped nations, but also to take steps to put the West in as good a position as we can to supply the necessary help.

The United States of America are sharing in this immense undertaking of the advanced world to help to raise the level of education in the developing countries. However, not being a former colonial power, the U.S.A. is not able to place at the disposal of the new nations the same large number of experienced advisers as Europe. With regard to the required volume of technical assistance the U.S.A. is doing everything with an enormous enthusiasm and altruism to create a large force of advisers. In connexion herewith I must draw attention to the Peace Corps. It is not at all my intention to ridicule this Peace Corps, but I believe that it is necessary to warn against the risk of paying too much attention to numbers, thereby underestimating sometimes the exceedingly great value of long-term experience in development problems as well as the necessity to use well-experienced teachers for the training of the volunteers of the Peace Corps.

On August 9, 1962, President Kennedy said in Washington, talking to trainees of the U.S. Peace Corps, that by the end of 1962 more than 5,000 Peace Corpsmen, men and women of all ages, will be serving abroad in all parts of the world, in countries about which most Americans knew little ten years ago, countries which they did not even know existed 20 years ago. With all sympathy and appreciation for the Peace Corpsmen, we cannot lose sight of the fact that the Europeans already knew these countries for centuries and had a very deep knowledge of all their human and material resources. Mr. Shriver, Director of the Peace Corps, has said: "Youth is not a liability for the Peace Corps or for our country. It is a great asset. The Peace Corps is fortunate to have placed instructors of approximately 25-26 years of age on the faculties of various universities around the world".[25] He considers that someone of 25 years is not too young for such a heavy task and points to the fact that the Minister for Economic Development of Tunisia is only 32 years old.

In my opinion this proves that the value of experience has been underestimated. It is logical that the new nations have to charge very young people with an enormous responsibility, but in the advanced world it will be more exceptional that a young man is placed in one of the highest functions and furthermore in that case he would have been selected out of a very large number of intellectuals and really has to be an outstanding person.

Not only young men and women, but also elder people are sent out now by the Peace Corps and increased attention is paid to the fact that the volunteers need a thorough training and briefing. I would like to warn against spending too much money on projects which are not essential for economic development. What is one to think about a request from a West African nation asking for skilled outboard motor repairmen who can organize a motor "bank" to keep fishermen operating after their motors have had a breakdown? This is a request that will be met by the Peace Corps.

25. R. S. Shriver, The job was tough, Article in Vital Speeches of the day, April 15, 1962, p. 40.

Furthermore we read: "Though interest in sports in Colombia is high, qualified instructors are scarce. The Peace Corps project aims to boost Colombia's sports programme by working directly with Colombian youth and by training Colombian instructors to take over after the volunteers leave".[26]

Taking into account the importance of technical assistance and the funds needed for the various programmes, it would be better not to waste people or money on a job which can easily be taught to a man of that West African state or on sport in Colombia as long there are still many more important problems to solve.

The great value of the Peace Corps is undoubtedly that more Americans are getting familiar with the conditions, culture, way of living, outlook on world affairs and so on in the underdeveloped countries. It may improve the understanding by American politicians of the different appreciation of certain world problems by European statesmen.

I have paid a lot of attention to the technical assistance given to the independent new nations by the West, but the activities of some governments to raise the level of education in their overseas provinces or regions for which they are responsible must not be belittled or even . . . criticized. At the present, in the case of Portugal, there are about 2,500 African students following courses in the Portuguese universities, of which about a third are from Angola. They will form the nucleus of an élite which will play an increasingly prominent part in the genuinely multi-racial society of Portugal (metropolis and overseas provinces) and this élite will increasingly represent the coloured people in the higher echelons of the civil service and the professions. All the Angola deputies in the National Assembly at Lisbon are natives of Angola, the majority of them coloured. We cannot compare the relations between the former Western colonial powers and their colonies with the situation in the entire Portuguese society. In all Portuguese territories, contrary to what has happened in most of those countries which regard themselves as paladins of the independence of peoples and equal rights for all with disregard of the colour of their skin (sometimes only theoretically but not in practice), racial or religious differences have never given rise to any discriminatory incident or measure in Portuguese society! The coloured population of the Portuguese provinces are assured by this attitude of a harmonious and rapid improvement of their living conditions. Why should we disturb this development of Portuguese society, wherein the chances for a rise of prosperity for all are promising. Where there is no race

26. Peace Corps News, May 1962, Vol. 2 No. 4, p. 2, and September 1962, Vol. 2, No. 7, p. 2.

distinction, we should not create a chaos like we have unchained in Congo, just to please a very small group instigated by foreigners unable to settle their own affairs in Africa.

The measures taken by the government of the Union of South Africa to give technical assistance to the new independent Bantu nation Transkei, although following different methods from the Western nations or the multi-national organizations, need to be appreciated in view of the existing local circumstances.

The underdeveloped world needs the technical assistance of the white people and as long as the coloured people obtain more prosperity, whether in an independent country or, for example, by the Portuguese system of interracial co-operation and reciprocal understanding, it has to be regarded as acceptable. History has shown that the high-flown slogans of fanatic leaders have never resulted in much good to the world!

My talks with people of developing countries have proved that they feel it as a slight discrimination to be equipped with young advisers lacking the required experience and wisdom of life. I really think that it is high time to establish a board or organization that must be charged with a very efficient and thorough selection of the people to be used as advisers in the technical assistance programmes. It might result in the creation of a large and well-experienced but also denationalized team of advisers with such a flexible mind that they are able to fit in well with the conditions of an underdeveloped society. Special attention has to be given to the attitude of the adviser. He ought not to serve the multi-national organization or his own interest, but to sacrifice himself for the good of the underdeveloped country to which he will be sent. We have to build up a corps of crusaders of the twentieth century to create prosperity and reciprocal appreciation—in freedom—in the developing world! Very often one can hear in the Western world that we—the white people—are civilized and place our culture on a very high level, giving rise to a feeling of superiority. However, there is not such a large difference between cannibalism and the slaughter in the two world wars or nuclear destruction. It is also questionable whether our culture with pin-up girls, hysteric jazz-sessions and so on, really is superior in comparison with the life and culture of the coloured people. I hope that the interracial aspects will settle fairly well and will be still better by the advance of time. The idea that a negro student cannot be allowed to study together with his fellow-students at the same university is out of date and a shame. It only proves that some white people are inferior to the coloured, as they have lost sight of the basic principle—the equal rights of the human beings!

The argument, often heard, that the developing nations have a preference for advisers from countries not belonging to the group of former colonial powers will do not here. The number of British and French advisers in former colonies of these countries is countless, but also people of other former colonial nations are working as advisers in private investment projects in underdeveloped countries with enormous success. Very often it shows that these advisers, sent out by private firms, have a considerably larger experience and work more efficiently than those of the United Nations. In connexion with this, I would mention the fact that the United Nations experts in the field of technical assistance are mostly surrounded by a large number of people in charge of their housing, transport and all other kinds of social affairs. The lamentation of the developing countries is very often that the group of attached people is larger than that of experts, but also that too much money made available for the technical assistance programmes is used for the well-being of the experts or for the administration of the multilateral organization charged with the technical assistance programmes. For example, the "administration costs" of the U.N.E.P.T.A. amounted to 19% of the sum made available for technical assistance. Efficiency is not the strongest point of most of the multilateral organizations and it might be useful to pay more attention to "Parkinson's law".

The developing countries are often critisizing, that a considerable part of the aid funds are spent on a too ambitious set up of the technical assistance team and therefore in their opinion spoiled. Sometimes 25-40% of the technical assistance team has an administrative or supporting task for the benefit of the whole group (reporting, housing, transport, foodstuff, social entertainment, etc.). The costs of the local labour and various facilities have to be paid by the countries receiving technical assistance and this is, with regard to the luxurious set up of the organizations, burdening heavily the national budget. It means that the total of aid and counterpart funds are not used in the most efficient way in the benefit of the developing country.

As we have seen, education plays a very important role in the development of a country, but many people think that development without addition to capital is impossible. The well-known economist Colin Clark, referring to the result of the investigations of a Norwegian colleague, wrote: "Dr. Aukrust found that he had enough data to permit a statistical estimation of the contribution of the different factors to real national product in Norway between 1900 and 1955. With no additions to capital at all, and no change in the labour force, "human factors", i. e., better knowledge, organization, skill, effort, education, enterprise, etc., sufficed to raise productivity at the rate

106

of 1.8 per cent per year. A one per cent addition to the labour force, all other things being equal, would only raise national product by ¾ per cent; and a one per cent addition to capital stock by only 0.2 per cent". Referring to his own investigations Colin Clark said: "A higher marginal return to capital, and a lower but still substantial return to "human factors", is shown by an analysis of the data for all the countries for which we have information. The "unspecified factor" is found to raise productivity on the average by 1.3 per cent per year. A one per cent addition to capital stock raised product by 0.47 per cent (other things being equal); the corresponding figure for labour is 0.42 per cent. It must be remembered that these are combined results for countries in a very wide range of stages of economic development. For the wealthier countries, in more recent times, a higher rate of return to labour and a lower rate on capital would probably be found".[27]

This proves that the developing countries are already able to promote their own development considerably, independent of the flow of foreign capital. However, the lack of a sufficient number of skilled people and intellectuals will make it difficult to follow the Norwegian example unless foreign experts are brought in, and the chance for this is given by the technical assistance programmes.

The leaders of a few new nations, although lacking the required well-trained people, are of the opinion that the technical assistance is used to influence their international state of affairs. In connexion with this, I would like to draw their attention to the fact that the governments of the underdeveloped nations are absolutely free to decide whether they like to accept technical assistance or to refuse it. They are also free to decide whether the foreign experts will fulfill a post in the government organization or will confine his activity to advice. Practice in Ghana has shown that the Communist experts have taken un unfair advantage of their position in order to influence the internal political situation. The President of Ghana took the required and well-known action. I think that it will be difficult to provide any example of interference in the internal affairs of any underdeveloped country by one of those sent out in the Western scheme of technical assistance.

This leads me to another aspect of technical assistance. However valuable it may be to send out teachers and advisers to the developing countries, it should never be forgotten that they have to be backed up by scientific research institutes which have collected an enormous

27. Colin Clark, "Growthmanship", Hobart Papers No. 10 of the Institute of Economic Affairs, p. 34.

wealth of information in connexion with culture, religion, traditions, social stratification, tropical diseases and so on of the under-developed population, and have also numerous resource surveys. Some institutes have had as their main field of activity the study of the methods for increasing the quality of tropical agricultural products in order to enlarge the crop and improve its quality. They were charged with this job in the colonial period and most of them still exist. The difference for them between the past and present is that they have got more experienced investigators (not forgetting the numerous re-patriated colonists) at their disposal, but the elimination of coloni-zation has resulted for most of these institutes in a decrease of avail-able funds. However, most of these research institutes are of the highest value for the developing countries as they generally are better docu-mentated than the new nations themselves. The major part of these institutes are located in Europe and that means that Europe is best equipped with the knowledge needed for a sound and scientific tech-nical assistance programme, and is also able to place the most ex-perienced advisers at the disposal of the developing countries. It will take years till the United States of America has built up a corps of really well-experienced advisers for technical assistance equalling in this respect in numbers the European potency.

In several countries official departments and sometimes even min-istries have been established, charged with the organization and co-ordination of the technical assistance and assisted by numerous private institutes and associations. It may be regrettable that there is too little co-ordination between the advanced countries. The available human resources of the Western countries are not being used in the most efficient way.

Although numerous multi-national organizations are dealing with technical assistance, I would like to draw attention to the bilateral technical assistance provided by the governments as well as by private firms.

In principle I have no objection to charging multi-national organ-izations with technical assistance as long the Communist countries do not belong to those organizations. Practice has shown that the Communists are trying too often to use technical assistance as a means of influencing the national policy of the new nations under cover of the flag of the United Nations. I have not the slightest objection to charging the United Nations with aid in the case of pestilences, famine, disasters (earthquakes, floods, etc.), but in the case of technical assist-ance there is too much chance of misusing this to meet political ends. As long as technical assistance is kept outside the political sphere and interests, any organization would be acceptable, but unfortunately practice has shown that we cannot trust the Communists in this respect. It is for this reason that I have an outspoken preference for a free-world multi-national organization charged with technical assistance.

This does not mean that I would like to eliminate bilateral technical assistance. In certain circumstances bilateral technical assistance may even be preferable, both from the point of view of efficiency and that of the "experienced expert". The interest in a certain project might be much better. In any case co-ordination of the technical assistance, whether multi-national or bilateral, is necessary. If everybody is planning and advising on his own, the whole thing becomes a mess. Too often the head of a local commission has to admit, when all the work is completed, that altogether it was really just an academic exercise and could not be taken seriously. That is a waste of effort and of the taxpayer's money in the advanced countries. Very instructive may be the following paragraph in an E.E.C. report of May 10, 1960/VIII/2496/60-H: "Millions of dollars have been invested in low-income countries without adequate knowledge of their resources or the priority with which they should be developed. Millions in public capital have gone into countries where there were not people trained in the technical, managerial and vocational skill required to carry out development projects. Such investment could not be fully effective. What is more, many additional private millions would have been invested—and would now be producing wealth—had the feasibility of profitable investment been revealed by greater pre-investment work over the past decade".

In the case of bilateral technical assistance much attention is paid to the selection of the adviser and very often we see a close co-operation in this respect between the private firms. Sometimes the government not only stimulates but also supports such private initiatives. An example thereof is to be seen in Germany. The "Deutsche Stiftung für Entwicklungsländer" is preparing carefully all those going to underdeveloped countries to make them familiar with the problems and the conditions they will meet. Most of the former colonial powers have all the means to do the same, and most of them are working on the same lines for the people they use for their bilateral technical assistance programmes. However, the United Nations, in their endeavour to send out as many people as possible to the developing countries, are not paying the required attention either to such private initiative to the bilateral technical assistance, although they increase the so badly needed potential of technical advisers. That attitude gives cause for serious criticism on my part. The present demand for technical assistance by the developing countries is too large not to make use of all available resources, as long as they are acceptable for the receiving nations and respect their sovereignty and independence.

Our conclusion must be that technical assistance, filling up the lack of required skill in the developing countries, is the determining factor for their rate of growth to maturity!

Chapter VI

THE FORMS OF AID

The controversy between East and West, the demand for a certain assortment of raw materials and tropical agricultural products and the search for new markets, have placed the underdeveloped countries in the centre of interest of the advanced countries. The colonial period has practically come to an end and has made way for the "period of rising expectations".

However, it is much easier to force plant growth in glasshouses than to develop the backward nations to the stage of maturity of the advanced countries. The majority of the nations of the underdeveloped world is increasingly insistent on asserting their independence and prefer to dissociate themselves from the tension between the West and the Communist bloc. They are using this controversy to play the blocs off against each other and are inclined to press for the channelling of aid through multilateral institutions that would not be able to apply pressure on them. Bilateral aid opens the possibility that the direct providers of aid will apply pressure on them, but on the other hand the developing nations are increasingly taking it for granted that aid and technical assistance will keep flowing their way, without any compensation. Humanity being what it is, one must doubt whether its sense of one-sided aid is as yet a powerful enough argument for this purpose. Both the endeavour towards prosperity and the development of population in the Western countries, and the endeavour towards political influence of the U.S.S.R. and Communist China, will be at a certain moment limiting factors with regard to increased or even continued aid, if there is no sign of compensation. I think that there will come a moment when the developing nations have to make their choice between economic co-operation and trade with the West and becoming a satellite of the Communist regime. Making a comparison between the amounts of aid given by the West and the Communists, as wel las the division of the aid amongst the underdeveloped countries, will teach the developing countries to know which side is accompanying most of its aid programme with political motives! In Chapter VIII will show the importance of private investment, which will have a still greater accelerating effect on economic growth and progress than aid and

111

also provides more suitable jobs for the increasing "élite" of the new nation. This additional flow of capital must not be underestimated by the underdeveloped countries, which are just in such a need of capital, both for the building up of their infrastructure and for their economic potential.

It is understandable that the government of an underdeveloped country seeks to receive grants or funds on subsidized terms instead of obtaining the required capital on market terms. However, in view of the capital required for a rapid economic development of the new nations, that demand can never be met only by the aid programmes, and taking into account that the donor countries must assert whether the size of the aid is consonant with their economic, social and political objectives and the governments have to render an account of their grants to the tax-payers, private investment will always have to be welcomed. Refusal of the latter will retard economic progress and in view of the expectations of the population for increased prosperity, such an attitude may be fatal for the government of a developing country. It is not at all imaginary that the donor countries will reason at a certain moment that aid given to a country stimulating private investment in order to accelerate economic progress, as is the case for example in Liberia, Libya, Mexico, etc., is the best way to spend the country's money made available for aid. Aid wasted in one country is aid denied to another which might be more conscious of the value of economic co-operation in a free world. The psychological effect of giving too much aid to an underdeveloped country might discourage the recipient government from promoting the inflow of private funds but leads also to a less conscious spending of the grants, as well as to inefficiency and a strangling bureaucracy.

The basic principle of all the Western multilateral or bilateral programmes of aid to underdeveloped countries is to accelerate their economic development up to a point where a satisfactory rate of growth can be achieved on a self-sustaining basis. Self-activity has to be shown and it will invigorate the mind of the donors to know that their aid is being exploited to the utmost to build up a well-balanced economy. The function of outside capital made available to developing countries is not to raise the standards of living there, but to offer the recipient nations a chance to build up their infrastructure. Aid will and must have a direct and indirect influence, when properly used, as it will promote the increase of the national income, savings and finally investment. It has no sense and it will never be the aim of aid to equalize incomes in different countries, for it is only given to have a catalytic effect. Continuation of aid ad infinitum will paralyze the energy of the people of a backward country instead of stimulating their self-activity. Once they have got the tools (in the form of a certain inflow of foreign capital), they are able themselves to increase their national income.

In the past a good deal of economic aid has disappeared en route. The administration and the inefficiency of the United Nations and its subordinate organizations have swallowed up large sums of money, but some of the aid has also gone into the private pockets of rulers and others in the recipient countries. As a result of poor planning and reports of inexperienced advisers, some plant and equipment has rusted away because nobody afterwards knew how to assemble or use it. A number of electric cranes, granted by the Netherlands government, have still been waiting for years on a quay of a Pakistan port to proceed to their destination. A lot of multilateral funds have been spent on projects which are not of any direct value to the economy of the developing country, and it has yet to be proved if they will do so in times to come. I have already mentioned the fact of the establishment of a cement factory near Abadan, costing the United Nations about $ 35 million, using for the present no more than 20 to 30% of its capacity. The lack of political unity has very often influenced certain projects. Some national authorities in developing countries are influencing the location of a certain project in order to stimulate to the utmost that part of the country where the people of their own tribe, race or religion are settled. There was a plan for the establishment of a sugar factory in Sudan. Climatic conditions were most favourable for sugar cane in the southern negroid part of Sudan, where the factory could produce for at least 7 months per annum, and then not only meeting the national demand for sugar but also allowing a limited export of sugar. On the advice of a "United Nation expert" a Sudanese authority of Arabian origin managed to have the sugar factory established in the northern Arabian part, where the climatic conditions for sugar cane were must unfavourable. I need not explain the result.

I may also refer to the way India has used its aid for the establishment of some over-ambitious heavy industries and is now facing serious balance of payments problems. The government now fears that the present "five year plan" will fail. The Minister of Finance is travelling around Europe like a beggar to obtain an increase of aid or soft loans. Most developing countries and not least India were very nationalistic and over-sensitive with regard to their independence and national pride, but I think that the mission of the Indian Minister of Finance—the logical result of disharmony in

113

economic development planning and over-estimation of the country's potential—is doing more harm to the national pride than the acceptance of sound advice from Western experts. Economic aid does not just subsidize people, it influences events, and if the aid is not used in the proper way, those events may be frightening, because the expectations are not met and the mistakes cannot be rectified at short notice. The developing countries have to understand that they must keep in constructive contact with the experienced advanced countries for their own benefit. The plans for economic aid are able to make and to maintain constructive contacts and to create working partnerships which are able to promote peace, respecting each others independence and liberty.

The whole process of economic development and progress requires an enormous inflow of capital. For that reason, the developing countries must realize that aid can and never will be a true substitute for trade. This applies both to the advanced and to the developing countries. To be valuable, aid must be a means of promoting the establishment of those essential undertakings which are indispensable for an undisturbed economic development. The new nations have to get familiar with the hard realities of the economic process of the world as it is. Therefore they also have to appreciate the aim of all aid programmes and of technical assistance, namely to construct a dynamic society, continuously absorbed in fruitful partnerships with other nations and other peoples. Today, economic forces and motives are a unique and essential element of the course of history and the developing nations are not able to withdraw themselves from the role they have to play in the history of the world.

The need for capital by the developing countries, disregarding the stage of economic growth they have reached already, is so great that nobody can deny that every help in this regard must be welcomed. The principle of the United Nations, excluding private investment as an important form of aid, proves that there exists in that organization a lack of knowledge with regard to the economic process of our modern world, or that this ostrich policy is followed on ethical grounds, neglecting intentionally the reality of world affairs. Anyway, I am strongly in disagreement with this principle of misjudgment of private investment as an important means to promote economic progress in underdeveloped countries. The United Nations are not consistent and in fact illogical, as they have no objection against long-term loans by the World Bank or any other multilateral organization on purely commercial terms! Like the United Nations, many people seem to fear that bilateral aid and technical assistance, just like private investment, will promote closer ties between advanced and developing countries. The most silly arguments are used to give the monopoly for aid and technical assistance to underdeveloped countries to the United Nations or any multi-national organization. Hoffman writes: "The principal reason why multi-national organizations such as the United Nations can operate more effectively is because the less developed countries prefer to deal with them, hence their bargaining position is strong. This means that they can insist upon maximum self-help from the recipient countries. This is important not only from a standpoint of cost but also because when the receiving countries become deeply involved in projects they accept responsibility for them. A further reason for lower costs and effectiveness in execution is that the U.N. has the whole world to draw on for its experts".[28] Indeed, in the case of bilateral aid or technical assistance the donor countries will mostly only give aid for projects fitting in well with sound development programmes and then also furnish really well-experienced advisers. With regard to the uninterrupted changing of the advisers and the officials of the United Nations organization, it is my firm belief that the effectiveness in execution, but also in supervision, of development projects and the use of grants will be of much higher quality in the case of bilateral aid. Well-experienced advisers, not worrying about their next appointment and selected by their government, have much more self-interest in the success of the project they are responsible for than any U.N. expert. In the case of bilateral aid we may expect that the people are also more cost-conscious for the benefit of the underdeveloped and the donor country!

Too many people think that it is our duty to spoil the people of the developing countries and that we only have to please them, although they are making the biggest mistakes at their own expense. We have to teach them the value of money, and that will be better for them than to make spongers of them. They will only reach maturity and their independence will only be a reality when they have learned to accept full responsibility for their own social, economic and financial existence. They need our aid, but they also have to understand that the Western tax-payer has to work hard to make the funds available for the aid programmes.

It is not at all my intention to propagate a new system of colonialism or trusteeship, but only to point out the necessity to teach the new nations how to survive and to safeguard their existence, just like parents do for their children. It may be worth while to cite Barbara Ward: "The peoples of other lands have been drawn into

28. P. G. Hoffman, Operation Breakthrough, Article in Foreign Affairs, October 1959.

the world economy created by Western enterprise. As their involvement increased, they, like the workers of the West, demanded enfranchisement and are now receiving it. But the last act is missing. There is no guarantee that after receiving the freedoms of the modern world, they will share more fully in its benefits. On the contrary, the first consequence of enfranchisement may well be to bring to an end even the remarkable chapter of direct assistance to their colonies which the Western powers began in 1945. Independence may well entail less stability, less prosperity, less work, less promise. It may end by being not the crown of a fruitful association but the signal of an increasing relapse!"[29]

However, the West and not least the former colonial powers have the firm intention to prevent such a relapse by an adequate aid programme!

Very often people understand by "aid" both financial aid and technical asisstance. Financial aid will very often be linked with technical assistance in order to make sure that the funds are used properly, but in my opinion we have to make a clear split between these two activities. For that reason we covered the aspects of "technical assistance" in the preceding chapter.

Financial aid to the underdeveloped nations may be given under different conditions. When we speak of aid to the underdeveloped countries, we are referring only to those parts of capital which normal market incentives do not provide. Governments of developing countries not respecting private capital and private investment, and nationalizing without a fair compensation, must fear that the foreign capital inflow will not be much higher than the amount of aid. Private capital will have an outspoken preference for countries respecting the rights of private property and civil law !

For our purpose we can distinguish aid now as follows:
a. grants;
b. interest-free loans (short- and long-term);
c. soft loans (including those repayable in local currency);
d. hard loans.

In all cases the financial aid can be tied or untied. When the aid is tied, it means that the receiving country has to respect certain conditions. It may be that the aid is given for a defined project or purpose, or that the aid is meant to enable the receiving country to buy the required raw materials, foodstuffs, consumer or capital goods only in the donor country.

29. Barbara Ward, India and the West, London, 1961, p. 95.

The receiving countries will have an outspoken preference for untied grants, both because they will not influence the economic policy of the nation concerned (sometimes with the danger that they will flow into the pockets of a few) and because there will not be any control on the spending of the money. Too often we are able to ascertain that untied grants are used for the most expensive "toys" on the markets or in other words for projects not fitting in with the short-term economic interest of the receiving country, based on the odd idea that only the very best will do, although the required skilled labour to handle the "toy" properly is lacking. As I mentioned before, we have to bring the people in the developing countries to understand that wealth and prosperity are only obtained with the utmost exertion and that their economic progress does not depend alone on the size of the grants they are receiving but also on their own efforts to improve their economic system.

The developing countries too often have the idea that the advanced countries have the holy duty to grant them large sums of money. Too often they are strengthened in that line of reasoning by the United Nations. But they have to realize that they must also take an active interest in protecting the balance of payments of the donor nations and that for that reason bilateral grants or soft loans sometimes have to be tied. It is easy to point to the wealth of the advanced countries and to blame them for selfishness, but although a country can be very rich, its balance of payments can be so vulnerable that is has to be very careful when giving money away. Lack of knowledge with regard to economic matters has resulted very often in dishonest remarks with regard to certain forms of aid. Schonfield gives a good example of this: "Unsophisticated people are easily obsessed by prices; they have even been known to argue that food which they obtain from the U.S.A. under their surplus disposal programme might have been obtained at lower cost elsewhere —regardless of the fact that the standard American practice in a poor country nowadays is to turn at least four-fifths of this "loan" into a gift. They do this by taking the local currency which is paid to them by the receiving country for the food, and giving it back to the government for use in its development programme".[30] The building up of the infrastructure of an underdeveloped country requires an enormous capital. On the condition that the infrastructure plans are sound, the advanced countries are willing to give them aid in the form of a grant. I am thinking in this connexion of the construction of a road system, a water-basin for better irrigation or a harbour,

30. A. Schonfield, The attack on world poverty, New York, 1960.

and not forgetting education. These are national projects yielding profit to the entire population and national economy. On the other hand there are certain infrastructure projects which are in the long run increasingly revenue-producing, such as railways and electric power stations. The investments to establish the latter are mostly a too heavy financial burden for the government of an underdeveloped country and therefore foreign aid will be required. However, it is questionable whether they should receive an untied grant, a grant with the condition to reserve out of the revenues for future repair or renewal of the unit, an interest-free loan or a soft loan. Personally I am most in favour of the three last-mentioned forms of aid for the reason pointed out above. Ideally, grants should be allocated where they will have the highest catalytic effect of promoting additional national effort or where the infrastructure would be crippled by lack of funds, but not to raise the income per capita available for consumption, as the latter would not shake the population out of its lethargy and would not stimulate their own effort to improve the living conditions. Such investment in economic infrastructure results directly only in a very small increase in income, but it is of fundamental importance to the profitability of more directly lucrative subsequent investments. Moreover, the advanced countries would never be able to raise the income per capita by grants to a level that would be worth mentioning.

I am fully in disagreement with Professor Friedman when he alleges that all economic aid should be stopped on the ground that in the long run it will almost surely retard economic development and promote the triumph of Communism.[31] Education in the science of modern economics, not forgetting in that connexion to explain the importance of trade and private enterprise, besides the technical assistance of really well-experienced financial advisers of the West, will satisfy to let them judge for themselves. Now already enough leaders of the new nations are well aware of the real intentions of the Communist aid and react accordingly. They begin to realize that Communist aid is primarily intended to serve political intentions. With regard to capital aid to the underdeveloped countries, I would like to sound a warning. The absorptive capacity is of crucial importance. The lower the level of development the more education and foreign technical assistance will have to precede the inflow of capital. The country's technical absorptive capacity must be decisive for the inflow of capital as this capacity relates to the possibility of using capital productively. The more harmoniously the economic

31. Prof. Milton Friedman, Article entitled: "Foreign economic aid: means and objectives", Yale Review, June 1958, Vol. XLVII, No. 4.

growth takes place the better. Capital aid must be offered to those countries where there is reasonable assurance that it will be used effectively, but assurance of continuity of aid is then just as important as the amount of aid. This may be a strong argument for correcting the system of co-ordination and co-operation as well as control of the aid given by the Western countries. Too much aid has been tied to certain projects. It is a big mistake to give a grant to one specific project only, as long it is not projected against the whole development programme. The various projects, being integral parts of a development programme are interrelated and reinforce each other. If this is not the case, the whole development programme will be thrown out of balance. It is for this reason that the most experienced advisers have to be sent out for technical assistance and always for a long period, but also that there exists a centralized organization informed about all aid-activities, whether multilateral or bilateral, in the form of grant or loan, tied or untied and so on.

Sometimes representatives of the new nations are visiting the capitals of the advanced countries, one after another, to ask the respective governments for aid or more aid on top of the funds already obtained from multi-national organizations and by that increasing the total inflow of capital in their country. As long as productive use is possible and is also made of it, the only objection one can make is that with regard to the total amount of aid made available by the advanced countries, the division of capital may be thrown out of balance. It is not always that the leaders of underdeveloped countries try to obtain as much inflow of capital to build up a strong and powerful nation and that they are able to make really productive use of it, but sometimes they spend the money on just a few impressive projects so that they can prove their national independence and prestige with visible symbols.

Nobody can deny that the spending of $ 12 million and $ 10 million respectively in Liberia an Ivorycoast for the construction of a presidential palace is irresponsible with regard to the need of capital for the development of these countries and this example proves that the leaders of new nations have not that conception of the value of money that is required to take full responsibility for the division of the aid they have obtained from the advanced countries. It proves also the indispensability of technical assistance, not with the purpose of influencing the national policy but to safeguard the right spending of the aid dollar. Channeling aid into uneconomic projects will easily subvert the economies of the underdeveloped countries instead of strengthening them and may ultimately result in dissatisfaction. Then the blame for the retarded progress will be thrown on

119

the advanced countries and particularly on the Western countries. Therefore it is in our own interest to make sure that aid is given where it is really required for economic growth and based on a sound programme. For that reason it is necessary that the people who have to advise on the desirability of a grant for a certain project, are well informed about the state of affairs in the country concerned, the economic development programme, but have to be themselves also fully qualified to give the correct judgment.

The faster tempo of financial commitments but also experience in the past has forced the World Bank to create a special branch for the preparation of development projects. The Bank has taken its responsibilities very seriously and has therefore agreed to share the cost of hiring and maintaining the best outside talent available to carry out some 10 studies in fields of interest to the Bank or I.D.A. The scope of the Bank ranges from technical and economic feasibility studies of individual projects to complete surveys of transportation, water resources development and the like. The Bank has been very selective with regard to the choice of her investigators and thus was able when taking a decision for aid, to pay full attention to the three sides of economic development, viz. projects, planning and policy. Plans and projects have always been checked and co-ordinated with the possibilities of the underdeveloped nations as they existed, with what the governments really wanted in the way of growth and change but also with what the underdeveloped country was prepared to sacrifice.

The World Bank has neither been in favour of amateurism nor welcomed everybody who liked to volunteer without a thorough selection. Some leaders of underdeveloped countries are of opinion that the World Bank is taking its duties too seriously and dislike that, but they have never been able to blame the World Bank for subjectivity or lack of interest into their problems. The big problem is that underdeveloped peoples often find the inhumanity of the market not only hard to bear, but even hard to understand and for that reason they also find it hard to appreciate the seriousness and objectivity of the World Bank. Here we are faced with the main problem of the aid to the underdeveloped countries. The conjunction of a large, more or less primitive sector with other rapidly advancing sectors (the Western countries) explains to a large extent the anachronistic coexistence of the backward and the modern world, too often resulting in a misunderstanding of the attitude of the Western countries.

The underdeveloped countries are too often not familiar with the fact that the governments of the advanced countries are also restricted in their possibilities to raise the amount of aid.

120

As I mentioned before public funds of the advanced countries have to be given as grants to the underdeveloped countries to build up their infrastructure. Private capital will practically never be made available for infrastructure projects. In the past years the Western countries granted the biggest share of the aid in order to develop an adequate roadsystem, to build harbours, hospitals or schools, but all the aid of the advanced countries together did not create sufficient sources of prosperity, employment possibilities and so on. The bilateral or multilateral grants and the bilateral interest-free or soft loans have been of high value for the building up of the infrastructure. The World Bank and the international capital market have given loans for a large number of self-liquidating projects, but only for well-selected projects not entailing too much risk. However, too little capital has been available for profitable undertakings. The economic but still more the political risks were too high. Although the I.F.C. has done a good job, it was not enough from an economic point of view to achieve a harmonious economic development of the new nations.

The governments of the advanced countries are not able to use public funds for such profitable undertakings in the developing countries. All they can do is to propose to their parliaments to raise the amount of aid for infrastructure projects. The economic potential of the Western advanced countries is to a large extent in the hands of private trade and industry. There is such an opportunity for private investment in the advanced countries and especially today in view of the rapid technological progress, that there is not very much interest for investment in the developing countries. This does not mean at all that there are not enough profitable projects available in the developing countries, neither that there should be an unwillingness to invest in the new nations, but the existing risks are making private investment too often less attractive. The required inflow of capital in the developing countries results therefore in a demand for increased aid out of public funds available to the governments of the advanced countries. In my opinion an increase of aid out of public funds of the advanced countries is needed and possible, but this increased aid should be tied to no revenue-producing infrastructure projects. The underdeveloped countries have to learn and to understand that economic growth can only be obtained by a well-balanced combination of public and private capital. Capital accumulation by itself is not the solution. Indices of the volume of investment in a country do not give a trustworthy indication of its prospects for economic progress and expansion. The majority of people in the Western advanced countries will not be in favour of spending public funds on profitable projects (with the exception of projects of general interest such as railways, electric power stations, gasworks and so on), which could be financed with private capital. The Communists are following their political and economic system, preferring to finance all economic activities only with public funds and banning any form of private enterprise. It is for that reason that they will be in favour of extending the activities of the governments of the developing countries also to projects which we prefer to reserve for private enterprise. The governments of the new nations have to blame themselves for the lack of interest in private investment in their countries. In many developing countries there is a considerable inflow of private capital because the investors know that their rights are respected. In the following chapter we will pay full attention to private investment and the aspects thereof.

There exists today a great demand for inflow of an increased amount of foreign capital and instead of promoting and facilitating private investment, the governments of some underdeveloped countries are now trying to obtain this capital by loans of the World Bank or other multi-national organizations whether of the governments of the advanced countries on a bilateral base. But even so the inflow of capital is deficient as the governments of the advanced countries are also restricted in their possibilities to give loans on a large scale.

There exists the danger that the government of an underdeveloped country, in order to keep all economic activities in its own hands and then not tuning the inflow of capital (by means of soft or hard loans), with the real demand for capital with regard to the economic development, are accepting a too heavy burden on the national economy. Black gives a warning in this respect: "A developing country can reach very rapidly the prudent limit of its capacity to assume fixed foreign exchange obligations, as we are learning in the Bank (I.B.R.D.). To ignore this prudent limit and simply pile loan upon loan is to destroy the very order in international financial transactions which development policy is in part designed to preserve".[32]

Aid can be tied or untied. I have given enough examples to prove that in several cases it is necessary to tie aid to a well defined project. When we see how the royalties paid by the oil companies to the oil producing nations (and it is a matter of millions of dollars) are benefiting only a small group instead of raising the prosperity of the whole population, we are warned not to give untied aid too easily. In the case of the oil royalties it is impossible to exert any influence on the spending of these huge sums of money for the benefit of all. As I mentioned

32. E. R. Black, The diplomacy of Economic development, Massachusetts, 1960, p. 55.

above there are also good exceptions, but a primary condition for giving an untied grant or loan is that there should at least exist an élite having the right sense of responsibility towards the population.

Grants and loans may be made multilateral or bilateral. The developing nations show a preference for multilateral aid. The receiving countries do not like to be linked by economic ties to a Western country. Very often they have no fear in this respect of Communist aid. It shows how shortsighted some leaders of the new nations are. The reason may be the fear to get involved in the East-West controversy or the idea that the donor country might influence their internal affairs. Others prefer multilateral aid in order to escape a too severe control on the spending of money, especially where some multinational organizations do not have at their disposal enough qualified people to pay full attention to the right use of the aid.

The Marshall aid from the U.S.A. to Europe after the last war proves that receiving aid need not at all affect the independence of a nation or its social or economic system. The American aid to Europe was partly tied to certain purposes among others to build up the defence. This bilateral aid has not influenced the sovereignty of any of the European countries. In our present world situation it is unthinkable that any foreign power (it may also be a former colonial power), will get a chance to influence the internal affairs of one of the new nations without its own agreement. World opinion would be upset if any Western nation should try to attack the sovereignty or independence of any new nation by economic pressure. Certain aid may be given or loans may be made on condition that they are spent on certain goods, such as capital goods, supplied by the aid giving country. The aid receiving country might have been able to buy similar goods more cheaply elsewhere, so that what it gains on the swings, may be lost partly or entirely on the roundabouts. In the case of a loan the borrowing country is completely free to accept or to refuse the loan under such a condition. When it concerns aid, the receiving country is also free to refuse tied aid. The receiving countries can never say that they are forced to accept aid under any condition, but it is possible that the need for inflow of capital should force them to accept those conditions, not being able to obtain the required capital elsewhere. There is too often a tendency to declare that the donor countries should only give aid and that they have no right at all to make demands or at least that it is unfair to combine the aid with certain conditions. The donor countries have the right but also the duty towards their people to safeguard their own prosperity, employment, balance of payments and so on.

As a result of this the government of the donor countries may give their aid partly a multilateral and partly a bilateral character, depending on their own economic position. When bilateral aid is tied, the reason for that may be to safeguard full-employment or to support their own capital goods industry by creating a new market. In view of the fact that capital is scarce and that the demand of the underdeveloped countries is so great that it cannot be met entirely by untied grants or loans, the receiving countries must realize that they must also understand that tied aid might be in certain cases the only method to increase the total amount of aid to them. Just because capital in the more advanced countries can be used more profitable in the advanced countries themselves, tied grants or loans to under-developed countries are in any case given with a certain loss of profit and unquestionably with a much higher risk. The attitude of a number of underdeveloped countries towards tied grants or loans is sometimes very unfair. Too often they refuse also to make a comparison between the amount of tied Communist aid and that of the West.

The purpose of aid to developing countries is to raise the income per capita. The capacity to repay the obtained loans should not be assessed by a static projection of the actual situation, but has to take into account the increase in income as well as the increase of savings which are the result of implementing a thoroughly worked out devel-opment programme. Grants and loans, especially with regard to the limited size of them, will only have a small influence on the rise of income per capita. Only private capital investment will be able to result in a considerable increase of the income per capita, in countries not having the Communist economic system and respecting private business to a higher or lower degree. Higher incomes make possible an increased amount of saving and investment and that are the only means to economic progress. It may be worthwhile to cite Benham with regard to the fact that the developing countries are often com-plaining about the aid received. He writes: "The maximum probable increase in economic aid to most underdeveloped countries is very unlikely to be a substitute for self-help and in any event nearly all such countries have development plans which depend mainly on their own efforts and resources, to which external aid is only a sup-plement".[33]

The Indian Ministry of Finance put forward the desirability that a larger part of the loans should be untied. They pointed out the frequent occurrence that new factories financed with "tied loans" could not work at full capacity because it was impossible to import

33. F. Benham, Economic aid to underdeveloped countries, London, 1961, p. 97.

124

the required quantity of raw materials. This example proves how sometimes the truth is twisted. The Indian government paid, through its ambition to become in the shortest possible time a big power, too much attention to huge projects and this upset the balance of payments which resulted in a shortage of foreign exchange. Poor development planning and too much ambition led to the acceptance of tied loans, which hampered these factories from working at full capacity. Instead of seeking the origin of the trouble in its own attitude, India is blaming the providers of the "tied loans". Ingratutide is the way of the world! Nevertheless the Western countries are striving now for more aid to the underdeveloped countries. As I said above, there are strong arguments for bilateral aid and that should never be forgotten by the receiving countries!

It is not only philantropy that has brought for example Great Britain and France to give so much aid to their former colonies. Even if these new nations do not form part of the Commonwealth or the Communauté, they receive a considerable amount of aid and technical assistance. The economies of both these two advanced countries and their former colonies, are so interwoven that it is to the benefit of both parties to maintain workable economic partnerships in undisturbed independence. Apart from the defence problems posed by the existence of Communism as a world power and apart from the strategic consequences thereof, the Western nations, and especially the N.A.T.O. countries, have given aid to the underdeveloped countries without any condition that could be linked with strategic or political purposes. All the Western countries are looking for, is to safeguard their own economies. In view of the East-West controversy they have to maintain their prosperity in order to be able to finance their defence. Progressive industrialization and the development of population have led to an enormous increase of trade within the sphere of the advanced countries of the West. The demand for capital goods was increasing more rapid in the advanced countries than in the developing world (see figure XI). The procentual composition of the world demand shows also a very remarkable trend. The demand for raw materials and basic metals is decreasing and that may make the advanced countries less dependent on those from the underdeveloped countries. The demand for capital and consumer goods shows a relative much larger increase in the industrialized countries than in the developing nations (see figure X). The conclusion we are able to draw from these facts is that, although the demand for capital goods is highest in the advanced countries, there exists an enormous market for capital goods in the developing countries. The massive demand with great purchasing power of the advanced countries is

125

of high value both for the advanced countries themselves and for the developing countries.

Although the intertrade between the advanced countries covers the majority of world trade, for the reasons we mentioned before, the developing world is also of high value to them. It is logical that a large number of the industrialized countries are in favour of bilateral aid in order to find new markets.

The competition on the markets of the developing countries by the advanced nations proves that the Western world has no political intentions with their multilateral aid, neither the preference for bilateral aid. The Soviet bloc on the other hand shows no sign of any form of competition on the markets of the developing countries. The only competition the Communists show on the markets of the developing world is that with the Western nations. The Appendix presents a survey of the contributions by N.A.T.O. countries for bilateral and multilateral aid and technical assistance in the years 1959, 1960 and 1961. For these years a subdivision is made in different categories, according to the usual way of splitting up the international flow of capital.

It might be useful to compare the official contributions to the U.N. agencies for multilateral economic and technical aid. The Sino-Soviet bloc aid is sinking into nothingless in comparison to the N.A.T.O. aid for official multilateral use.

The foregoing may show the developing countries which of the two opposing blocs of our world is using most the multi-national organizations. Considering the competition on the markets of the developing countries and the flow of capital to multi-national organizations, both by the N.A.T.O. countries and the Sino-Soviet bloc, it cannot be difficult to find which bloc is giving aid primarily for political ends! The Appendex shows also the enormous effort made by the former colonial powers for the multilateral as well as all the other forms of aid to the new nations.

As has been said above there is in the Western world a marked preference for bilateral aid and technical assistance, given to the various underdeveloped countries in order to serve the national economy. Figure XIII shows the increase of bilateral aid and technical assistance (both public and private) for the whole of N.A.T.O. A spokesman of the West German government said recently: "The rule of thumb with regard to German aid will be: multilateral aid as much as necessary, bilateral aid as much as possible". This is also the rule of thumb of all the Western countries. Although the total multilateral aid is small in proportion to the total bilateral aid (10% in 1959, 15% in 1960 and 13% in 1961), we have explained

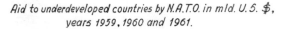

Aid to underdeveloped countries by N.A.T.O. in mld. U.S. $,
years 1959, 1960 and 1961.

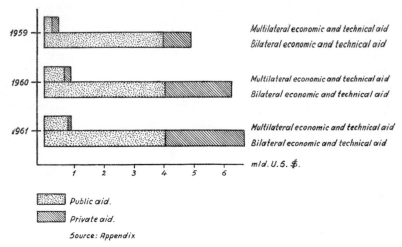

Public aid.

Private aid.

Source: Appendix

Figure XIII

above the importance of an increase of the total inflow of capital to the developing countries. Attention may be asked for the fact that the total amount of bilateral grants by the N.A.T.O. countries amounts $ 2,768 million in 1961 and that of the Soviet Bloc is estimated $ 900 million.

On top of this enormous bilateral aid to the developing world comes the multilateral aid of the N.A.T.O. countries in addition to the favourable influence of private investment.

The purpose of Western aid to underdeveloped countries is to keep in constructive contact with them but also to come to working partnerships, which will be likely to remain intact irrespective of the controversy between East and West. The Western countries have not the intention to draw the underdeveloped countries into the controversy, but they are trying to build up a free world—a shrinking world—wherein economic ties between the West and the developing world are promoting prosperity for all. The leaders of the developing countries have to face the realities of the world economy and to understand that economic co-operation is a must for both the Western countries and the developing world, and of reciprocal profit. Economic co-operation does not undermine sovereignty or independence. The developing countries are on the wrong track, when they think that they can isolate themselves from the effects of the economic forces ruling in this shrinking world. Peace will be served only by working partnerships with other nations. The new nations have got

127

a say in world politics by their membership of the United Nations, but then they must also accept to play their role in the economic system and organizations of the world.

The controversy between East and West is an inescapable reality. The only thing that can preserve peace is the possibility to get raw materials and markets by the N.A.T.O. countries to safeguard their peace economy and thus maintaining the balance of power between East and West. Peace means liberty and self determination and these are also goals of the developing world.

CHAPTER VII

PRIVATE INVESTMENT IN UNDERDEVELOPED COUNTRIES

Professor Tinbergen wrote in connexion with the developing countries: "For several reasons, it seems appropriate, in large sectors of the economy, to rely on private production and investment. It may happen, however, and it does happen, that private activity falls short of the most desirable level or is applied in wrong directions. Development policy therefore should include an elaborate system of stimuli and deterrents intended to provide some guidance to private activity".[34]

In a recent publication of the O.E.C.D. we read :"The magnitude of the official aid effort should not hide the usefulness of the contributions of the private sector to the economic development of less developed countries. Private investment has special advantages in the development of many sectors of the economy which do not receive public help. They may also contribute to the efficient use of capital and other resources. Although official contributions generally lead the way in providing planning, basic economic and social facilities and general technical assistance, there is a large and important role to be played by private capital both from foreign and domestic sources".[35]

I stressed the necessity of capital inflow in the underdeveloped countries in order to create a self-sustaining economy, but as I explained the financing of the infrastructure and most of the public utility services is swallowing all the public funds made available on a multilateral or bilateral basis to the developing countries. It will take decades before the latter are able to do without this foreign public aid. The two quotations above indicate the necessity of private capital flow. In a publication of the I.L.O. we find the following: "Private foreign capital can thus play an important part in developing industrial sectors in underdeveloped areas either in association with local enterprises or by establishing its own subsidiaries".[36] Rosenstein-Rodan writes: "Private investment should not be counted as aid".[37] According to

34. Prof. J. Tinbergen, The design of development, Baltimore 1958, p. 50.
35. Development assistance efforts and policies in 1961; (O.E.C.D.), 1962, p. 35.
36. Employment objectives in economic development (International Labour Office), Geneva 1961, p. 134.
37. P. R. Rosenstein-Rodan, The review of Economics and Statistics, Vol. XLIII no. 2, May 1961.

this writer private foreign investment is "trade not aid". With regard to the enormous lack of capital in the underdeveloped countries, although not covered by the common definition of "aid", I think I am not far wrong when I speak in this case of "trade being private aid".

Especially taking a view of the not inconsiderable risk of private investment in many of the underdeveloped countries, private capital inflow has in a way the character of aid as it may be revenue-producing both for the investor and the country where the investment has taken place. In several cases the investment will bear fruit only after years, but it creates from the very outset employment and influences the balance of payments in the underdeveloped country. Exploration and exploitation of natural resources (mining, making borings, etc.) require huge investments, but they will promote a diversification of exports, making the country concerned less dependent on just a few products. Figures VI, VII and VIII have shown that many underdeveloped countries depend on too few products, although they are rich in natural resources, which could not be exploited by lack of capital. It is true that the total quantity of raw materials, required by the advanced industrial countries, may decrease in the long run as a result of the discovery of synthetic plastics and fibres. However, there are also indispensable essential raw materials and, moreover, the demand of raw materials will increase as a result of the growing industrialization in the new nations and still more in consequence of the increased demand for consumer and capital goods by the developing countries themselves, which will in its turn influence trade within the developing world. Although for the moment the rate at which the demand for raw materials increases is less than the rate of industrial expansion in the advanced countries as a result of the introduction of artificial raw materials, there is an increasing demand in the entire world and there are promising developments for the not too distant future. The exportation of natural resources, so far now not used, may by exploitation as a result of foreign private investment become the pace-maker for the rest of the economy of the developing country. Therefore, why should a foreign public loan for the exploitation of a state-owned copper mine or oil well of a developing country be indicated as aid and not foreign private investment? Investment is the main factor in economic growth and is the primary condition for technological change, industrial organization and finally of world trade, but only when overall output increases more rapidly than the expanding of population in the new nations, is there a higher productivity and for all good management.

Foreign private investment will mostly go hand in hand with private technical assistance. After the last war West Germany was enabled

130

by aid from the U.S.A. to build up its industrial potential and these investments provided the country with the most modern technical capability, resulting to a large extent in the creation of the "Wirtschaftswunder". Foreign private investment in the developing countries may provide them with a modern industrial potential and that will consequently also accelerate the economic growth. Through this private technical assistance the new nations are becoming familiar with a large part of modern technological information and will promote as well the educational level because the foreign firms will make use of the local labour force. Private technical assistance provides very often specialized technical training for local workers. Many large foreign firms are building houses for their local employees and provide good social services for their workers and their relatives (medical treatment, schools, sports fields, etc.). Also it should be of great concern to the new nations, that foreign private investment provides (which is very important) many jobs for those of their countrymen who have studied at Western universities and for whom there are not suitable jobs available as a result of the low stage of development.

In my opinion the foreign entrepreneurs and investors are essential for the economic development of the underdeveloped countries and that development gives an excellent opportunity for middle class employment.

The breakthrough of Mexico from stagnation to rapid economic progress is partly due to foreign private and public investment.

The U.S. Undersecretary of State for Foreign Affairs gave a warning to the underdeveloped countries during one of the last conferences of the World Bank: "It may be thought by some, that a developing country should be able to look with confidence to a perpetual inflow of public funds to supplement its internal savings and thus feel free to discourage private investment. I think it may be said with absolute certainty that no developing country can safely make such an assumption".[38] The developing nations should come to realize that private investment contributes to local public revenue in the shape of export duties, income tax and so on. Private firms concentrating their activities on the export of raw materials or consumer goods (initially foodstuffs or plain manufactured national products such as woodcarving, textile products, etc. and later more complicated goods) are increasing exports and therefore foreign-exchange earnings.

The more the governments of the underdeveloped countries consider that steel mills, mines and sometimes even plantations should be owned by the State, thus hampering private enterprise, the more

38. J. Reston, On myths and realities of foreign aid. The New York Times, 19-9-1962, p. 4.

they are reducing substantially the scope of foreign private investment. And what is worse, they drain their public funds, which are already not sufficient to establish the very necessary public utilities and to build up the infrastructure.

Although purchasing power, obtained as a result of multilateral or bilateral grants or loans, is able to bridge to a certain degree the enormous gap between the developing countries and the advanced nations, it will never lead to a really satisfactory fundamental change in the national economy. Money is not the only mean of raising the income per capita or changing the social attitudes and institutions or the physical environment. The object the underdeveloped countries must have in view is the extension of their national economy in the overall pattern of world supply and demand. I pointed out the fact that a diversification of products for export is necessary, but to be succesful one has also to know the demand. Marketing is not an easy job and requires much experience. Experience in this field is what the underdeveloped countries are lacking and only foreign entrepreneurs are able to develop new markets for the products of the new nations. The bigger Western firms are mainly interested in investment in extractive industries, therefore in raw materials for the world market. However, a harmonious economic growth requires also the export of various other products. It will be known that there exists a dangerous and depressing lag in exports from the primary-producing countries (apart from the oil countries) in comparison with the export from the industrial countries. For that reason too much attention cannot be paid to all those measures, promoting an increase in the number of export products. The medium size foreign firms are just as important to the economy of the underdeveloped countries as the big companies. The foreign entrepreneurs will not only make the developing countries less dependent upon the export of just a few products, but their activities, besides promoting the diversification of foodstuffs and semi-industrial products, will also create a large number of additional economic activities within the developing country. I have in mind small factories for packing material, printing-offices, transport concerns and so on. The national or local market will, especially in the early stages of economic growth, be small and for that reason foreign private investment by the medium size or smaller companies will only be interested in export products, but their work will promote economic activities by the people of the developing country requiring only a small investment. We must not underestimate either the risk nor the difficulties the foreign entrepreneurs will face. Climatic conditions for manufacturing processes in tropical areas will be very often unfavourable. Although wages may be low in comparison with those in the advanced countries, the labour output may be low and costly air-conditioning installations will have to be used to raise the output. This may lead to a high cost of production and high consumer prices, making competition on the Western markets more difficult. On the one hand this proves that the economy of an underdeveloped country can never be identical to our Western economic structure, but on the other hand that the task of a foreign entrepreneur is not an easy one.

It proves also that the development planning requires experienced and well-qualified people, who are familiar with such problems. In some developing countries we have seen foreign private investment by international financial firms in plantations, where the direction was laid in the hands of one of the autochthonous nations.

The big problem of most of the underdeveloped countries is that they very often have to meet international competition and are entering into export markets which have established producers.

Should the foreign entrepreneurs become afraid of nationalization or confiscation without satisfactory compensation, or of difficulties with the transfer of profits or a restriction on the use of foreign experts when required, they will not be very eager to invest in a developing country with such an attitude and policy.

A problem for many of the new nations is the lack of a middle class, which is able to perform the entrepreneurial role and in such cases the foreign private investors have to make use of people from the advanced countries until they can be replaced by the trainees of the developing nation.

Trade is not a simple matter, particularly not for the unexperienced entrepreneur or exporter of a developing country. Through their lack of experience they sometimes blame the advanced countries for mistakes and losses. Frost, aware of this discontentment in the developing countries writes: "The efficiency of the market system or economic organization is not by itself a sufficient recommendation to the people of the backward countries. The market system may be efficient, but it is considered by backward peoples to be lacking in charm. It induces them to be precise. The market is impersonal. The valuations of the market are repugnant in more ways than only impersonal. They are depressingly precise!"[39]

Many countries depending to a high degree for their imports on the revenues of just one or two products, will have to face a number of difficulties in their balance of payments through a fall in the price of their products on the world market. However, there are also countries complaining about the prices on the world market because they

39. R. Frost, The backward society, London 1962, p. 90.

think that they have to be treated in a more special way and that the advanced countries have to pay them a higher price than that of the world market. They like to be subsidized in every way but in doing so they often misuse the aid they receive. They prefer the easy way of living and like to profit from the advanced countries without any compensation. It must be admitted that this is not the general attitude of the underdeveloped countries. Only a few like to play off East against West, without making a serious effort to increase their economic progress by their own means.

In all cases industrialization is necessary in the developing countries in order to break through the one-sided economic structure, but they must also realize that industrialization is not an easy remedy offering them quick prosperity and solving their social and economic problems. With all the techniques of the advanced nations it will not be possible to achieve an economic growth in just a few years in spite of foreign aid and technical assistance, and which took centuries before the Western countries could reach their present state of economic welfare. Foreign private investment and technical assistance are the only available means of being able to reduce the required time for reaching the economic stage of maturity. Even the Dutch Professor Tinbergen, well-known all over the world for his interest in the underdeveloped countries and strongly in favour of multilateral aid and technical assistance, wrote: "For understandable reasons there has been reluctance in some of the underdeveloped countries to admit foreign enterprises, and frequently such enterprises are regarded with suspicion: in the colonial era they often were the symbols of political influence. But this is no longer the case, in many countries, and the situation should be re-examined on both sides. The best thing to be done in the interest of both the underdeveloped areas and the private enterprises concerned seems to be a clear separation of political and economic considerations. Investment of foreign capital from the investor's side, should be treated as a purely economic matter, not influenced by any desire for political activity. Accordingly, economic policies with respect to such investments should be based, by the receiving countries, on their economic significance".[40]

The private investor is very often not at all in favour of political influences on his economic activities. On the contrary they are sometimes in conflict with each other. A recent example is the transportation of goods by the merchant navies of various N.A.T.O. countries to Cuba, although the U.S.A. was at the time in favour of a blockade for political reasons. Some N.A.T.O. countries gave advice not to

40. Prof. J. Tinbergen, The design of development, Baltimore 1958, p. 60.

134

transport Soviet goods to Cuba, but others refused to put political pressure upon the economic activities of their shipping companies.

Many underdeveloped countries lack the required entrepreneurial skill in their own population and in that case private enterprise is forced to send out their own specialists to give guidance. This private technical assistance is an expensive business and for that reason they will take those measures only, when the underdeveloped countries are unable to make available the required people with entrepreneurial skill.

By apprenticeship inside the underdeveloped countries the creation of an entrepreneurial "élite" may be promoted. This may be indicated as private technical assistance. Education and especially university teaching is not giving that entrepreneurial skill required by private enterprise. Experience in private business will be learned only on the job after years. This is not always well understood and too often people think that the education of entrepreneurs is a task of the government. Some people differ in opinion. I quote a conclusion in a publication by the European productivity agency of the Organization for European Economic Cooperation: "In view of the keyrole that governments have historically played in economic development, and because of the desire for accelerated growth, many participants expressed strong interest in study of the role that public investment may play not only in construction of infrastructure, but in industrial undertakings as well. It was pointed out that in Turkey the training of government officials to manage public industries has been a major factor in the creation of a skilled managerial group who in many cases have subsequently established key private enterprises. Where tradition, political uncertainties, social, cultural class structures and other obstacles to the growth of a vigorous private enterprise system may exist, an important impetus to development may be given by creation of public enterprises, which in some cases may later be sold to private interests".[41]

We are aware of the lack of capital in developing countries. When a government has to manage public undertakings as a result of obstacles to a vigorous private enterprise system, it means that less public funds are available for infrastructure and public utilities, which can never be for the common good. Furthermore, when a government had not done everything or was incapable of creating a normal and healthy society, wherein private initiative could have a fair chance, it does not prove that the training of government officials to become entrepreneurs is as a general rule preferable. Sometimes we see public

41. Regional Economic Planning, edited by W. Isard and J. H. Cumberland, O.E.E.C., Paris 1961, p. 424 and 425.

undertakings in many countries, including advanced countries, justified by the fact that the risk for private enterprise was too high but the undertaking nevertheless had to be founded in the interest of the national economy as a whole. Lack of entrepreneurial skill was not the justification for public undertakings and as soon as the undertaking was less hazardous for the private investor it was very often handed over. In my opinion the training of an entrepreneurial élite and a skilled managerial group is primarily a task for the private firms, while general education and university teaching is a concern of the government. Foreign private enterprise and technical assistance will promote economic growth, but activities of the government to train entrepreneurs and managers or to establish a public undertaking will retard economic progress (with the exception of the case mentioned above). Public investment and enterprise should be restricted to such projects belonging to what may be called "impulse sector". With regard to this subject, we subscribe to the following view: "Within the limits for total investment, and if growth of per capita income is the chief aim of development policy, it can be stated, as a general principle, that public investment should always be expanded at least to the point where opportunities for private investment are maximized".[42]

A passage in an I.L.O. publication is also interesting: "It is particularly desirable that foreign investors should be encouraged to employ and to train local staff including managerial personnel to sub-contract some processes to local producers, and to develop joint ventures with local entrepreneurs. A number of developing countries have already offered guarantees and liberal tax concessions to attract foreign capital and these may be adopted by others"![43]

It is regrettable that some developing nations are discouraging foreign private enterprise and a new Pakistan law gives a good example of such an attitude. An amount equal to 5% of the existing obligations to the foreign private banks in Pakistan at the end of the preceding year, and at least Rs. 2 million in foreign currency or equivalent securities, has to be given on deposit to the State Bank. Also the Pakistan government is allowed to forbid the foreign banks to accept deposits. The 21 foreign private banks are seriously hampered in their activities by this new law. On the other hand Pakistan is asking the advanced nations for an increase of aid for its second "Five Year Plan". It is questionable if the Western tax-payer will be

42. Programming techniques for economic development (report by a group), U.N. Economic commission for Asia and the Far East, Bangkok, 1960, p. 17.
43. Employment objectives in economic development (report of a meeting of experts), Geneva 1961, p. 133.

in favour of granting more money to Pakistan, when normal economic co-operation and private enterprise is made more or less impossible. One can have more appreciation for the activities of the Indian Investment Centre. This Centre investigates all demands for technical assistance and/or foreign private financial co-operation and makes selections. The aim of the Centre is to prevent requests being made world-wide for financial participation in undertakings which could have a bad influence on the reputation of India as a trustworthy country for foreign private investment. This Centre is a private institution, financially backed by the Indian government and assisted by foreign technical and financial advisers.

One may have less appreciation for the treatment of foreign private enterprise. The Indian government is levying taxes of 63% on outgoing dividends and royalties. We do not think that this is a very clever policy, as it will hamper the inflow of foreign private capital, foreign technical knowledge and the use of licences.

It is understandable, that the governments of the developing countries are not in favour of a considerable outflow of capital, but there are other methods than those used by Pakistan and India. On the Ivory Coast there exists a national investment fund. All firms are charged with a 10% tax on their profits, unless they are able to prove that they re-invested more than the 10%. This resulted in a rapid increase of foreign private enterprise.

Non-alignment is the general political course of most of the under-developed countries and that is fair enough, but when they also want prosperity, they must realize that foreign public funds are not and never will be sufficient to meet their need of capital and that foreign private investment is the only way to increase the inflow of capital in order to obtain prosperity within a reasonable space of time. It may lead to irritation, frustration or tension, when the people of the under-developed countries become aware that independence by itself brings little prosperity, but there can always be found a solution by which their independence is respected. However, the foreign investor is also entitled to a fair deal. Governments and private enterprise do not have conflicting interests; they must be partners in progress for the benefit of both. The governments of the new nations, especially when they have a shortage of skilled civil servants, should be very careful not to enter too much into the field of private enterprise. The Indian government has already a considerable number of public enterprises, but now we put on record increased activity of the State Trading Corporation. Private capital will benefit the country in which it is invested in various ways. However, investment in a developing country will be made primarily for the benefit of the foreign investor in the belief that the capital will yield a higher return than elsewhere. The less risk, the more the investor will be in favour of long-term private investment. He will anticipate the economic growth of the country. Long-term private investment is just what the new nations need for a harmonious economic growth, but it will also solve many balance of payments problems.

The treatment which a foreign private investor receives from the government of a developing country is sometimes very discouraging. Mr. J. Loudon, said in a speech entitled "Some problems of private enterprise in a divided world" to the Economic Club of New York on 6th March, 1962: "What is required—from both capital importing countries and from the foreigners who invest in them, is a far sighted appreciation of realities—in particular a realization of their mutual and interdependent self-interest. While the investor must of course pay the fullest regard to a country's national susceptibilities and problems, he is also entitled to a fair deal. He has a right to expect adequate safeguards for the security of tenure and service which governments may have made with him". I think this statement needs no comment.

Some countries are of the opinion that large foreign companies may interfere in their national, political and economic life. With regard to the power which the governments of the new independent nations wield (for example nationalization, expelling foreigners, blocking the outflow of capital, etc.) I think that the foreign investor has to fear more than the new nation. Therefore the fear of a re-introduction of colonialism through the backdoor in case of foreign private investment is unrealistic.

The developing countries, growing to economic maturity understand that such a growth cannot but result in a change of accent from aid to economic co-operation!

The big foreign companies, paying much attention to research and development, will not only be able to invest large amounts of capital in the developing countries, but they are handing over a managerial and technical knowledge of considerable value to the development of the country. An investigation in 1959 showed that the ratio between foreign and local employees in executive functions in British firms working in 17 developing countries changed from 5 : 1 in 1950 to 5 : 4 in 1958.[44]

Foreign private enterprise in an underdeveloped country is not at all an easy matter. The foreign entrepreneur is a stranger in a strange country and it takes some time before he can become familiar with the language, the tradition, the temperament, and the way of life, but

44. A. J. Guepin and others. De taak van Nederland ten aanzien van de ontwikkelingslanden, Haarlem 1962, p. 60.

he will meet many more difficulties when he has to find his way through numerous government offices to obtain the required information, licenses, approvals or assistance. The foreign entrepreneur needs not only patience, but he must also be a diplomat and a psychologist.

Klineberg wrote about the foreign adviser: "The expert is usually a capable engineer or educator or agriculturist; he is not always capable of dealing with human beings of a different culture, or of adapting himself—or his family—to life in a new cultural setting. It is not easy to specify what qualities of personality are required, but it seems highly probable that among them, as a minimum, there must be freedom from ethnic prejudices and from authoritarian attitudes, there must also be flexibility, empathy (the ability to place oneself in the position of others), and a concern for the welfare of others."[45] Most of the big European Companies, working in the past in the colonies, now have experts at their disposal, who possess that experience which is needed today for the difficult task in the developing countries. Practice has shown that mutual interest, co-operation of the national and foreign entrepreneur where there is sharing of capital and management (joint enterprise), will lead to increased success. Above I have stressed the importance of foreign private enterprise in the underdeveloped countries, but in my opinion it is necessary that the latter try to build up as soon as possible their own group of enterpreneurs. Co-operation with foreign enterprise may accelerate the growth in entrepreneurial skill. President Tubman is strongly in favour of this mutual co-operation and proves it by the following words: "I told you at one time that we did not need aid, just all the co-operation we could get. It is for people like that, regardless of race or color, that our door is open. Wide, wide open. We still need all the co-operation we can get, and now, more than ever, we are able to co-operate".[46]

With such an attitude, which we can only applaud, progress in the developing world will be eruptive without being disruptive.

Joint ventures, undertakings whereby capital, management and entrepreneurial risk are spread over the participants—the foreign investor and the underdeveloped country or his national investor—will promote reciprocal understanding and interest. I refer in connexion with joint ventures to an American study by W. G. Friedman and G. Kolmanoff, entitled "Joint International Business Ventures" (New York, 1961) which gives the arguments for and against "joint ventures".

45. O. Klineberg, A psychologist's approach to technological change, International Social Science Bulletin, VII, 3, 1955, p. 349.
46. G. Scullin, A visit with W. V. S. Tubman, President of Liberia, Think, June 1962.

If industrialization in the developing countries is to succeed to any substantial extent, a considerable adjustment between the use of the machines and the habits of the local labour is of primary importance. The succesful mixture of these unknown and often contradictory elements requires an amount of diplomacy and knowledge of the foreign and national entrepreneur or manager.

In my opinion this kind of co-operation between the West and the developing countries, with all the risks therein, will help to sweep away to a large extent the fear of a re-entry of colonialism by the backdoor, but also that feeling of inferiority. The Western countries will then be able to deal with them as equal partners.

Foreign private enterprise in developing nations has been in itself an underdeveloped field, although it is in my opinion one of the most stimulating forces to accelerate the economic growth in the developing free world.

CHAPTER VIII

THE DEVELOPING FREE WORLD

In the preceding chapters I have used the designation backward, underdeveloped or developing country intentionally not in any order. In this chapter I would like to show very briefly the differences in development both in various countries and in areas of the developing world.

The countries comprising the Sino-Soviet bloc are not free in their political and economic behaviour and for that reason there is no point in discussing their problems or their stage of economic growth. Their future will be determined without their consent by the Communist leaders in Moscow or Peking.

The governments of the new countries of the free world are able on the contrary to take any decisions they think best for their people. They may make mistakes, but they will learn from them. Experience is the best teacher! By that experience they will gain a better insight into the political and economic aspects of the free world.

The distinction between "backward", "underdeveloped" and "developing" may appear at first sight rational; however, it is neither fair nor correct and in fact even misleading. One country may have a very weak economy for lack of enough natural resources but may possess an élite able to develop the country successfully as soon as the required capital is available, while an other has a tremendous wealth in natural resources but lacks the people needed to make use of this wealth. The natural resources in the Congo are of high value, but the élite in the country is very small, as there are no more than 40 Congolese who have finished their studies at a university.

In some Latin American countries there is a true copy of the Spanish or Portuguese society, although the income per capita is rather low, while there is still an archaic society with many tribes in some new African nations, possessing an enormous wealth in natural resources. There, the leaders of the tribes are now the new political leaders, but—as is the case in the Congo—they all find their own political supporters only in that region where their own tribe forms the majority of the population. Under such circumstances political unification will not be reached in a short time. The social structure in the less-advanced countries plays a very important role. In India, where the original social structure was still intact, and the average educational level was not too low, an important élite was available and it was not too difficult to take over from the British after independence was obtained without creating chaos. The first decision of the new Indian government was that all British laws and regulations for India, should remain in force for the whole of independent India.

In some countries we will find that certain regions have already reached a high degree of development, while others are still completely archaic. We find in some new nations a number of very modern cities, while a hundred miles away the most primitive conditions still exist and the chief of a tribe is ruling his community in the same way as his ancestors did many centuries ago.

The average income per capita of a nation may look very satisfactory but sometimes such a country has still to be classified as backward. In the chief oil-exporting countries the present revenues from oil are so large that the average income per capita would justify the conclusion that these countries do not need much aid. However, the revenue from oil is not used to promote the economic development of the country and to increase personal prosperity, but are only enriching a small group. Aid to such countries would not be of much help to the poorer class of people. The set of laws and the political structure of a country considerably influence the possibilities of development. The more archaic the political structure, the more difficult it will be to obtain a change in the division of prosperity. It is not true that the possession of large natural resources is in any case the primary condition for economic growth. Many agrarian countries show a higher incomer per capita than nations with much natural wealth.

Professor Haberler remarks that 14 Far Eastern countries account for about 40 per cent of the world's total of cows and buffalo's, but only 10 per cent of the world's milk output. From a purely technical view point, there is room here for great improvements, without large capital outlay, by changing methods of production and breaking down old-fashioned prejudices. The solution of the problem is by no means easy, but the bottleneck is not the availability of large capital sums but the redirection of government activities.[47] Nor is the density of population a trustworthy indication of the chances of development.

I hope the reader will accept that I shall henceforth use the general expression "developing countries" and shall use "backward country"

47. Humanity and subsistance. Article from Prof. G. Haberler. Population pressure and economic policy. Annales Nestlé, Vevey 1960, p. 105.

only when the nation concerned is still really in the early stage of economic or political growth.

In passing I would like to add that at present there is not available in the economic theory any really trustworthy yardstick to compare the degree of prosperity in the various developing countries. In determining the differences in prosperity, it is not only necessary to construct a price index for comparison of income between rich and poor countries, but also for the latter, based on a standard commodity group of international validity and also taking into account such factors as climatic conditions, religious rules, etc. For, without any generally accepted yardstick it will be impossible to compare the various stages of economic growth but such a yardstick is also indispensable for sound planning of the development of the young nations. I do not think that Bernstein's definition is either satisfactory or accurate. His definition is: "The best test of an underdeveloped country is its level of real income and the rate at which per capita real income is increasing. In short, an underdeveloped country is one in which output per capita is relatively low and in which productive efficiency is increasing very slowly, if at all".[48]

It is beyond the scope of this study to give a complete description of the politico economic situation in the various developing countries or even in the larger areas of the free world, such as Africa, Asia and Latin America. I will confine my remarks to facts of general interest, influencing the relations between the new nations and the N.A.T.O. countries.

There is no sense in plunging into history; we are interested only in our present relations with the developing countries in order to create a situation in the free world wherein reciprocal economic co-operation is possible for the mutual benefit all concerned, but also to the benefit of N.A.T.O. defence, being for the moment the only power able by its "force in being" to preserve peace.

We have reached a new stage in economic relations among the countries of the free world and history has never shown such a widespread effort to help the less fortunate people. In some cases it will be much easier to accelerate the economic growth than in others. Social structure, large differences in wealth, religious prejudices, political structure, lack of unification, too little diversified production, climatic and geographic conditions, and similar factors, are different in the various developing countries. On the whole, and only with a few exceptions, it may be true to say that Latin America is the

48. E. M. Bernstein, "Financing economic growth in underdeveloped economies", in "Savings in the modern economy," ed. W. W. Heller, Minneapolis, 1953, p. 267.

part of the developing world which has the best chances for a relatively rapid economic progress. By pausing to review the developing parts of the world, requiring aid and technical assistance, I would like for that reason to start with Latin America.

In every respect there are large differences between Latin America and the other de-colonized parts of the world. In the past colonization in Latin America by Spain and Portugal resembled the system of colonization of the ancient Roman Empire. Most of the Roman sprawling was intended to be permanent; the colonization became migration on a large scale in order to create a colony, with much resemblance to the status of a province. Later not the autochthonous population but the colonisers made themselves independent of the Spanish or Portuguese motherland. The result was that the colonisers together with the autochthonous population fought for their independence. The attitude of the former colonisers to the native people was completely different compared with that in Africa or Asia. The natives were welcomed as equal citizens, although in the lower sections of the population, the condition was that they became Christians, thus creating a more or less harmonious population. Later the former Spanish colony fell apart in several independent nations. As a result of this course of history the Latin-American communities are showing a resemblance to the Spanish or Portuguese societies. Brazil became first an empire and only in 1889 an independent republic. Despite the fact that the Latin American countries obtained independence at such an early date and with an élite to form an able government, the economic development was very slow. The growth of Latin America was hampered by innumerable revolts. Public and private armies often became the final arbiters of political matters while generals exploited public discontent. Militarism in Latin America today is a cultural residue of the Wars of Independence and the subsequent civil disorders. Even today when the low prestige of the armed forces causes them to withdraw from active political competition, they will remain instruments of power and political factors. Functioning as veto groups, they will be in a strong position to preserve their privileged status and to protect the relatively large share of the national budget they receive in most of the countries.[49]

Although the basis for economic growth is available, Latin America still belongs to the developing world as a result of the existing political disequilibrium.

Illiteracy in Latin America is still high and amounts to 45 per cent

49. The role of the Military in underdeveloped countries, edited by J. J. Johnson, Princeton 1962, p. 93 and 125.

although this figure is slightly better than in Asia (65 per cent) and Africa (80 per cent). These figures are averages and the percentages are different in various countries. In Argentina the percentage amounts to 13.3 per cent and in Brazil 51.4 per cent. Therefore all attention must be concentrated on education of the mass, considerable decrease of the income gap per capita, dynamic improvement of agriculture and development of the backward regions by construction of a widespread transport and communication system. All this is needed for most of the Latin American countries. I have come to the conclusion that we need not fear communism in Latin America, but when the poorer masses are not supported by the Western countries in their move to improve social security and prosperity, they will be thrown into the arms of Communism. Fidel Castro became a hero in the eyes of the poorer masses of the other Latin American countries, promising a rise in prosperity by land reform and all kinds of social reforms. In this way he became a Messianic person to the poor people of South America. I do not underestimate the political problems, but in my opinion we will invite a most serious civil war in Latin American countries if we do not take the required measures at short notice to support the moderate powers in these countries in their move for social reform. Cuba is the writing on the wall of what to expect, when a conservative group hampering a progessive social policy for its own benefit, is supported by the West. The poor people will blame the U.S.A. and other Western countries for the continuation of the absolutely unacceptable living conditions. They will look at the slogan of the "Development Decade", as launched by the Secretary-General of the United Nations and taken on by the advanced countries as an expression of the desire to help the developing countries, as meaningless statements. They will praise Fidel Castro not as a Communist, but as the champion of the interests of the poor and then accepting Communism into the bargain. Latin America is not struggling with a density of population at the rate we see in Asia and for that reason we can be rather optimistic with regard to the development of this part of the world. Nevertheless we must not underestimate the danger of the enormous difference in wealth between a small group and the majority living at a minimum subsistence level. The social circumstances may result in serious internal political difficulties. With all due respect and appreciation for President Kennedy's "Alliance for Progress Programme" and the "Charter of Punta del Este", all attention should be given to improving the living conditions of the mass of the population. We have to realize that there are in existence some small but very powerful groups of wealthy people, hampering the increase in prosperity of the mass of

145

the population. The foreign policy of the West and particularly of the U.S.A. has to be concentrated on this problem. There is a social revolution going on in Latin America and we have to support actively not the conservative group profiting from a continuation of the out of date social system, but the moderate social reformers.

The strength of this social revolution is shown in an article of Grubbe. He spoke with six presidents and a large number of ministers of Latin American countries concerning an attack by the U.S.A. on Cuba. They all declared that they would have to disassociate themselves from that American action, in order not to be eliminated immediately by their own people.[50] This story proves how delicate is the political situation in Latin America and shows the growing influence of "Castro-ism". For that reason I would like to warn against too much optimism with regard to the approval the U.S.A. received from the governments of the Latin American countries when President Kennedy started the blockade of Cuba. The above mentioned article underlines the need to increase the prosperity of the poorer masses of Latin America as soon as possible and to transform the dictatorships into democracies.

Berle, an expert on Latin American affairs, wrote: "What we are seeing now is a group of twenty independent Latin American states in all of which attempts are being made to disrupt the present social order by supposedly revolutionary forces which have yet to demonstrate capacity to construct anything effective in the place of the formations they destroy, and whose chief emphasis is on combating the United States and entering the Soviet or Red Chinese empires".[51]

It is necessary for Latin America to undertake a profound technological revolution in all sectors of its economy. This is the only way to achieve higher levels of employment and real income and, concurrently, to solve first and foremost today's social problems and secure a sustained rise in living conditions. There must be an end to the existence of many dictatorships, which are attended too often with corruption. On historical grounds many people in Latin America are looking to the United States of America as the great power, which can influence to a large extent their internal affairs. The excessive anti-U.S.A. policy of Cuba still appeals today to some groups in Latin America and gives support to "Castro-ism". A number of Latin American dictatorships have taken extreme measures against national Communism. I do not believe that this policy will result in a long term solution, although it gave the re-

50. P. Grubbe, Der Schatten Kubas auf Lateinamerika, Aussenpolitik, August 1961, p. 530 and 531.
51. A. A. Berle, Latin America, Diplomacy and reality, New York 1962.

quired support of Latin America to the U.S.A. during the crisis in October 1962 concerning Cuba.

Although in recent years the nations of Latin America have become more closely linked through trade and investment than ever before, political relationships have become in certain cases more and more strained. The attitude of the political leaders of Latin American countries is not so important, but the attitude of the majority of the peoples of these countries with regard to the U.S.A. and the West is the decisive factor. For that reason much more attention must be paid to social reform and the increase in the standard of living of the poorer masses of Latin America. Without underestimating the value of industrialization, the primary task is rural development—involving land tenure; tax and fiscal policy related to land use; agricultural credit; programmes dealing with marketing, land reclamation, and productivity. This is also the area of social development which is indicated as of primary interest in the "Act of Bogota". The Act is in the form of a resolution which makes two broad statements:

a. That faster social and economic progress in Latin American countries is essential for the preservation and strengthening of free democratic institutions in this hemisphere.

b. That to achieve faster progress, greater co-operation among nations and maximum self-help will be necessary.

I think that the realization of (a) above needs priority, especially when one realises how many people are still living in houses which are made of petrol-tins or crates. One may say that the standard of living in Latin America is generally much higher today than two or three decades ago and higher in most parts of Latin America than in most of the countries of South East Asia and Africa, but that is an over-simplification! In view of the enormous wealth of small groups in Latin American countries, and the fact that the necessary élite and education was available during recent decades, a more rapid economic growth and an improvement in living conditions of the poorer masses could have been achieved. Mayobre wrote: "Most frequently, in the case of Latin America, the entire attention of the economic authorities is taken up by the problems of the moment. Whatever the reason, in many countries, the public action reflects a general economic, fiscal and monetary policy characterized by conflicting measures or systems of which the ultimate aims are not clearly distinguished and which in the final issue prove ineffective or prejudicial to the balanced development of the economy. Still more often does it happen that in some countries where there exists a desire and determination to promote economic development, the possible

147

effects of measures adopted to this end are weakenend or nullified by the counteracting influence of others."[52]

In the last decade Latin America has been an "underdeveloped area" in view of the programmes of aid and technical assistance of the multi-national organizations. This is the more regrettable as Latin America had available all the human and natural resources for a rapid economic development and could have been built up as a solid bulwark against Communism and a footing for international co-operation, not only within the Western hemisphere but in the whole free world. The U.S.A. and even Europe has an important task to fulfil in Latin America! If illuminating results in the Development Decade are to be obtained, anywhere it is in Latin America. Since most social reforms involve some redistribution of income from the wealthy to the poorer classes, they tend to increase total consumption-expenditures at the cost of savings and investments thus resulting in a slower growth of production per person. Capital inflow as a result of multilateral or bilateral grants, soft loans but also foreign private investment are needed to safeguard the economic development of Latin America.

Education of the lowest class of people must have first priority. There exist many universities with well-equipped laboratories and large sums of money at their disposal, but the number of primary and higher grade schools is quite insufficient. Western aid and technical assistance to improve the educational facilities in Latin America must be increased immediately.

Since the nineteenth century, economic development of this large part of the world has been based on the exploitation of natural resources. The vast majority of its exports is composed of basic commodities, but the production of industrial goods is now increasing. Figure VIII shows that in many countries of Latin America the revenues of one product very often make up more than 50% of the total export-yield and that is making these countries very vulnerable to changes in the prices of these products on the world market. Institutional factors, protectionist policies and other measures of the advanced countries are affecting too often the trade of basic commodities. The late Professor Nurkse has indicated some factors which have resulted in a lag in exports of primary products. One of the reasons appears to be, among others, a considerable substitution of synthetics for imported natural materials, but he also blames for this existing demand-deficiency a shift in the pattern of

52. J. A. Mayobre, Programming as an instrument of policy (Chapter in "Economic Development for Latin America", edited by H. S. Ellis, London, 1961), p. 30.

148

output in the advanced countries in favour of engineering, chemical industries and all kinds of other industries and services.[53] On the other hand there has also sometimes been a supply-deficiency. Haberler proves this with the following example: "The most extreme policy of discouraging agricultural production was pursued by Argentina under the régime of Peron. Prices paid to farmers were kept far below the prices paid by foreign buyers with the difference flowing into the coffers of a government export monopoly. This policy not only ruined the Argentinian balance of payments and greatly weakened the Argentinian economy, but also reduced world food supplies.[54]

Nobody will deny that, with regard to the balance of payments, a national economy depending upon three quarters of its exports on one product (coffee), as is the case in Columbia, is very vulnerable to any change in the price of this commodity on the world market. Negotations are now carried on by 36 coffee-producing and 22 importing countries (responsible for 95% of the world export and import) to stabilize prices and to agree upon the export quotas in order to help the coffee-producing countries. The same procedure will be adopted for some other commodities. Although this will be very important, it is not the best way to reach a long term solution for the balance of payments problems of Latin America and other developing countries.

It is shocking that a large number of people in Latin America are still going hungry. By education, modernization of agriculture, social reform and making full use of the available arable land the prosperity of the rural population may increase rapidly. A considerable percentage of arable land owned by a small number of wealthy people is not used, while millions of farmers are not able to feed their families with the harvest from their small areas of land. Nobody can blame them for being disgruntled with such an archaic system of division of land tenure. This type of situation resulting in a very low purchasing power is hampering industrialization in some countries as the national market is too small to take to mass-production methods.

One of the basic problems of Latin American trade is the fact that over 90 per cent of the total export consists of basic industrial or food commodities. World demand for these became less than the demand for manufactured goods. A drawback was also the concentration on just a small number of these food commodities. Not

53. R. Nurkse, Pattern of trade and development. The Wicksell lectures, 1959, Stockholm.
54. G. Haberler, Population pressure and economic policy, published in Humanity and subsistance, Annales Nestlé, Vevey, 1960, p. 105.

149

only a diversification of the export-commodities is necessary, but also a dynamic industrialization programme. Colombia possesses many natural resources and exploration as well as exploitation of those would result in the solution of many of the financial problems. The geographical location and the existence of good ports, together with a policy of the government to create a good climate for foreign private investment are promising for the future of Colombia. Most of the countries of Latin America have considerable natural resources and as a result a diversification of economic activities would not be too difficult. To carry its own weight in the world economy it is necessary that Latin America, besides its production of basic commodities, should pay full attention to a profound technological revolution. Industrialization is the only way to solve the present balance of payments problems of many Latin American countries.

To achieve higher levels of employment and income per capita not only is industrialization needed, but also a vigorous expansion of the infrastructure (education, energy, transportation, communications, etc.). The expansion of heavy industry and the production of capital and consumer goods is possible in most of the countries in this part of the world. Many of them also possess oil. Competition with manufactured or semi-manufactured goods with the more industrialized countries will not be easy. However, in the present stage, it is obvious that regional integration will make it possible for the Latin American countries to expand their markets reciprocally. A certain protectionist policy within the Latin American area is reasonable to give the young industries a chance.

A serious drawback for most of the smaller Latin American countries is that Western manufacturing corporations prefer to establish subsidiaries in the bigger countries which have larger and expending domestic markets. Costa Rica, Ecuador and El Salvador among others, despite the good treatment foreign capital is receiving there, are hampered in their drive for industrialization. Furthermore the smaller countries are handicapped by the fact that foreign private investment has a distinct preference for nations with rich natural resources and with expanding domestic markets. The relatively smaller countries like Nicaragua, Ecuador, Costa Rica, etc., are not receiving as a result of these factors sufficient financial assistance required for satisfactory economic development, in spite of the political stability in some of them.

Latin America can be the most promising area of the developing world, especially if the Western countries pay more attention to its development by increased aid and technical assistance! However, this progress will only be achieved provided there is political stability,

150

a sound social reform and a diversification of export products. To achieve a harmonious development of the whole of Latin America, the creation of a common market may be required in order to help the smaller nations particularly.

Next we will focus our attention on the Asiatic area. The Portuguese colonization was accompanied by migration intending to create overseas provinces. However, the colonization by the British and the Dutch in Asia about 1600 had the character of a settlement of a large number of factories (trading-posts), in which the latter exercised only partial sovereignty in the foreign country. This type of colonization showed a resemblance to the colonization system of the ancient Greeks. The main purpose was trade and the colonisers stayed in the outposts, but had little interest in the native society. All their attention was concentrated on trade and the safeguarding of the trade routes. It took more than two centuries before the governments of England and the Netherlands completely took over sovereign power. The French followed the British and Dutch example. The differences in administration of the colonies of England, France and the Netherlands were great, but they had a common policy of keeping the native society intact and migration hardly took place. The power of the native authorities and the hierarchy was unaffected. The colonial powers occupied themselves mainly with the improvement of agriculture, the promotion of trade and contacts with the outside world. I do not think there is any sense in describing here the differences in colonial policy of the three motherlands, but for our purpose it may be of interest to call attention to the fact that the preservation of the native social structure and the use of native people as low-grade government officials, facilitated the de-colonization and the taking over of government. A good factor was also that the colonial powers had paid attention to education and the creation of a relatively small élite. Nevertheless, the development in the new Asiatic nations shows a different picture. The leaders in independent India realized that they still needed the help of the United Kingdom and other Western countries to speed up the economic growth. Elsewhere fanatical leaders were of the opinion that after obtaining independence they were ruling a mature society and could do without any aid or technical assistance from the former colonial power. The result was chaos with the disintegration of important organizations, the nationalization of foreign private enterprises, and lack of qualified experts. These leaders did not understand and would not recognize that their behaviour only hampered the development of the country and would decrease the living standard of the people. It is too little understood by the new leaders that liberty and independence will

151

only become a reality, if their nations are able to create prosperity as a result of their own efforts and economic co-operation with the rest of the world.

India is respected in the whole world, despite the problems it is facing as a result of the development of population and the mistakes made by paying too much interest to very ambitious undertakings. The neutrality of India is respected and has not been influenced, but stimulated by the aid and technical assistance from the United Kingdom and other Western countries. Although India has not such a wealth of natural resources as Indonesia, it will be ahead for decades in political and economic development in comparison with the latter. Abrupt breaking of the ties between the new nation and the former colonial power results very often in a struggle for power between the native leaders and promotes corruption, which in its turn hampers a healthy development.

Just as in Latin America, the Asiatic countries are in need of capital for their economic development and besides multi-lateral and bilateral financial aid, foreign private investment is of great importance. The development of population is the most serious drag on accelerated economic progress. Reform of agriculture, industrialization, but also a change in traditions and religious rules will be necessary.

The Asiatic countries have not had the benefit of independence for centuries like the Latin American nations, but the existence of an ancient culture and an intact social structure will still prove to be also of great value. Political stability, the attitude against foreign private capital and sound development programmes will be decisive in the rate of economic progress. Co-operation between the Asiatic countries is just as essential as in Latin America. The economic and cultural co-operation between Thailand, the Philippines and Malaya in the Association of South East Asia is a great success and these three countries are showing the most rapid economic growth.

The countries of South and South East Asia have made substantial progress to which Colombo Plan activities have contributed.

Just as in Latin America, occasional setbacks occur with unfavourable weather-conditions and falls in world commodity prices.

The completion of the Chainat Barrage in 1957 in Thailand and construction of an irrigation system has added many thousands of acres. In India, additional irrigation facilities have been provided for some 18 million acres of land within a decade and furthermore about 4 million acres of waste land have been reclaimed. The Ghulam Mohammed Barrage in Pakistan brought in over 330.000 acres of land. Similar activities elsewhere have also decreased the general food shortage in Asia.

Rural community development projects have raised the level of agricultural techniques. Industrial development is planned, varying in rate and extent according to the particular conditions in each country, and the United Kingdom plays an important role in this respect by giving adequate technical assistance. In general, primary emphasis is laid upon the creation of basic facilities and services. Infrastructure projects have of course priority. As a result of the low purchasing power of the people, the home market for consumer goods is still small, but will increase through a rise in prosperity.

The countries of Asia which are members of the Consultative Committee of the Colombo Plan are encouraged to formulate development programmes based upon a realistic assessment of resources available. However, some countries and especially Burma and Indonesia, are still faced with problems not only of development but of rehabilitation of an economy disrupted by the Second World War, and internal political difficulties and strife.

It will be understood that the spending of a large percentage of the national income for military purposes, will retard economic development. Some Asiatic countries are forced to pay much attention to their defence, being threatened by the infiltration of Communist Chinese troops, but Indonesia's ambition to occupy Dutch New Guinea not only used up large sums of money for the purchase of military equipment but also created narrow political ties with the Communist world.

The use of multilateral and bilateral aid by developing countries, for military purposes, when not really threatened by aggression, can never be said to be properly used for economic development. The purpose of aid is to create prosperity and not political unrest.

Much that has been said in connexion with the development of Latin America is likewise appropriate to Asia. The most important differences between Latin America and Asia with regard to the chance of accelerated economic progress are chiefly the density of population per square mile and the political instability. The threat of Communist Chinese aggression, which is demonstrated regularly in the various countries of South East Asia and now on the borders of India, and also the political attitude of the Indonesian Government (the close ties with the U.S.S.R. and Communist China), are discouraging foreign private investment. The sometimes rather crude treatment of foreign capital in Asiatic countries may be seen as another drawback. Increased public aid to the co-operative Asiatic countries to fill in the lack of sufficient private investment is necessary.

Something must be said about the Middle East. The small basis of prosperity (mainly the revenues of the oil wells), the exceedingly complicated problems of the society, the corruption and the very often archaic political structure, notwithstanding the inflow of considerable foreign capital (royalties), are hampering economic development here. The standard of living of the poorer masses is extremely low and will create increasing political unrest. The West must do everything to create better living conditions in this area, because it is the cross-road between Europe and Asia. The problems to be solved here are extremely difficult, as the standard of education is very low. Diversification of export products will be difficult because the soil is not fertile, and the obstruction of the archaic rulers to political reform will sometimes be great.

Altogether, both Asia and the Middle East are developing areas, where economic progress, with some exceptions, will be very difficult and certainly very time consuming. It will be a difficult job to meet the "rising expectations" of the big poorer masses. Adequate development programmes will be needed and only those with experience and knowledge of the existing political and economic conditions can be used for technical assistance duties.

A bid for leadership in the Arab world by President Nasser of Egypt and the reluctance of the leaders of Middle East countries to recognize or accept his leadership creates much tension. Dreams of unification of the Arab world are cut short by the many preconditions. Tension is also created by the fact that some countries are fortunate enough to possess oil, while others are lacking natural resources or arable land and hardly know how to collect the means for an ordinary existence.

The differences in development and wealth between nations in the Middle East are enormous, but also between the various regions within some of these countries. In the modern state of Iraq, actually under-populated, we see the contrast of modern towns and the nomadic tribes of Bedouin with their flocks and camels. The prosperity of Iraq largely depends on the oil industry but it is still primarily an agricultural country. For the first time in nearly seven centuries the country is free from any outside domination or influence and under the new government the mass of people can be said to have a share in prosperity. Education is being given top priority and schemes for the expansion of light industries and infrastructure have been set up. Jordan on the other hand is facing severe economic problems hampering development. These differences in natural resources, arable ground, education, political structure, rivalry and so on, lead to tension and make it very difficult to construct a workable and reliable development programme for the Middle East. The situation in the Middle East is of an explosive character. It would be wrong and a misinterpretation if the West should try to change the political situation. In this case only multilateral action has a chance to create better living conditions in the poor countries with an increasing population and a low level of education. With the exception of the oil companies, foreign private investors are not very interested in this part of the world, threatened by revolution and political unrest and having for the moment a very small chance of succesful industrialization.

The main difference between Asia and the Middle East is the fact that, generally speaking, the social and economic conditions in the latter are really "backward". As mentioned before, the differences in the various countries are enormous. Feudalism still exists by the side of modern wealth with the result that some societies are living partly in the time before the ninth century and partly in modern times. The transition in this part of the world has mainly a political character and this is partly due to the artificially constructed nations after the last war. For example, Jordan lacks the required solid political and economic base and is able to survive only by the aid of the United Kingdom. After 1945 it seemed that the Arab League would solve many of the problems as the result of a move to unification, but afterwards the unifying power of pan-Arabism, pan-Islamism and a move to a fair division of wealth proved but an idle fancy. The clash was between the new political reformers and the historic leaders (kings, sultans, emirs, etc.).

The political leaders of the Middle East are not willing to recognize the hard fact, that the wealth in certain countries exists by the grace of the Western oil companies and their activities. Instead of co-operation, the Middle East is a model of jealousy and contrast, wealth and the most severe poverty; only the Koran and the Arabic language are the unifying symbols.

Africa is the third area of the developing world and the problems we are facing here are not less serious than elsewhere. In spite of the construction of a few harbours and a number of towns around the perimeter of the Dark Continent, Europe knew practically nothing about Africa until a century ago. The countries on the borders of the Mediterranean received the main interest of Europe as well as the Union of South Africa, but Central Africa remained an unknown and mysterious part of the world. Africa has been penetrated by the Semitic and Hamatic peoples and later by the Moslems. Empires were created and then vanished, but only the equatorial region remained the mysterious society of the Bantus. The jungle, the climate and tropical diseases presented a threatening barrier to the Europeans and this together with the lack of a road system and often hardly navigable watercourses caused that the white man penetrated to the interior regions of Africa only very occasionally. In 1855 during the Congress of Berlin the African territory was divided up amongst some European countries. Europe was interested only in the extraction of raw materials and the creation of a few markets. The result of all this was that only on the periphery of the African continent an elementary infrastructure was built up. The lack of a social structure or native political structure in the larger part of Africa did not create close co-operation between the Europeans and the Africans as we saw in the other developing nations between the colonists and the native people. These circumstances have enormously retarded the development and awakening of Africa as a whole. The European penetration in Africa in the 19th century, the industrial revolution in Europe with its increasing need of raw materials and even more the last world war have awakened an interest in Africa. But even today, much of Africa remains difficult to penetrate, whilst also a large proportion of its people as will now be readily understood has not had much contact with the outside world. From an ethnic point of view it would be a mistake to speak of racial divisions in Africa since all races are mixed. I will not review all the races of Africa, but it may be of interest to mention only the five major groups living south of the Sahara: Hamites, Bantu, Negroes, Bushmen and Hottentots. I used deliberately the word "group" instead of "race" as the determining factor is more linguistic than racial. In numbers the first three groups mentioned are the most important. The various groups (large and small) have not shown from the beginning of the drive for self-determination and de-colonization much interest in unification. Pan-Africanism was an imported idea as it was invented by expatriate Africans somewhere else in the world. The first native Africans becoming interested in the idea of unification were the tribeless people, who had settled down in the industrial towns. Both the lack of unity and tribal form of African society with its various groups combined with the absence of a social structure as we saw in the former Asiatic colonies resulted in a struggle in the sixteenth to the nineteenth century between the Portuguese and the Arabian kingdoms for the control of the coastal area of East Africa. From that time the Portuguese were in possession of Mosambique. The Arab occupation of Zanzibar, completed in 1840, was the last move of the Muslims into the north-eastern part of Africa. Indians settled down in the region between Kenya and Natal primarily as labourers. The Christian kingdom of Ethiopia is the last remnant of the penetration of the Greco-Roman world into Africa, but has shrunk enormously in size since those early days. The conquest and conversion of North

Africa and Egypt to Islam lasted until the twelfth century. These Islamic conquerors penetrated from the Sudan to the Middle Niger and by the way of the desert caravan routes to the upper Niger and to the Senegal river. The negroes of West Africa show a variation from tribe to tribe at least as great as that between Norwegians and Italians. Though their political unity was very rudimentary, in agriculture and crafts they were the most advanced of all the Africans. Here, in West Africa the European colonization took place.

A completely different picture is shown in the northern part of Africa (north of the Sahara), which in the second century B.C. was populated by Mediterranean peoples and Europeans. The Muslim states were later conquered and colonized by the latter. The largest settlement was in Algeria but in connexion with this it must be observed that also large numbers of Algerians afterwards settled in France.

In South Africa the Dutch settled in the seventeenth century, founded a white community and drove the Bantu to the north.

On the whole one may say that Africa is thinly populated and arable ground is available to a much larger degree, especially if the water-supply is improved and modern European agricultural methods should be introduced.

Having given a very general picture of present Africa one might remark that the political frontiers seem to bear little relation to the natural geographical areas, or to the cultural, religious or ethnic frontiers as they existed in the past. In connexion with the Europeans we have seen that they settled down only in the most accessible points of the coastline and established official colonies or commercial companies in the shape of a factory. In the last century very large parts of Africa remained untouched by any foreign political influence. The colonization of large parts of Africa by European powers must not only be seen from an economic point of view (trade) but also in the light of the struggle for the European balance of power. For the present the European interest in the development of Africa is two-fold, economic and political! The future of Africa does not only influence Europe, but is of worldwide importance. By worldwide we mean here the future of the whole free world! For that reason we have to pay full attention to the development of Africa, but we are facing many problems, completely different from those in other former colonies, which are at this moment in a state of such rapid political transition and influenced by a wide variety of factors, that even their boundaries are very difficult to estimate. We must not forget that (for most of their history) the African native inhabitants have lived for centuries under conditions of independence in the most extreme form which can be imagined. Economic development programmes for Africa have to take into account that a large number of Africans lived and very often are still living in small tribal societies separated from each other by sometimes even completely uninhabited regions, and with no contact worth mentioning with the outside world. The bulk of the African people still pursue economic activities based on subsistence production and even regional markets do not exist, owing to the natural barriers and furthermore to the lack of the most primitive form of infrastructure. Traditions frequently still play a very important role. In this respect Kimble liked to point out the fact that incentives resulting in increased efforts to raise prosperity in Europe, will have no effect in several parts of Africa. The efforts of the African élite in this respect are fruitless as a result of present indolence. The existing labour force is large enough, but the number of those willing to work for an improvement of the living conditions is small.[55]

Köbben has produced some characteristic examples. The Akim of Ghana are trying to earn enough money out of the cultivation of cocoa for the world market in order to have an easy life without work. A substantial part of earnings were wasted at funeral festivals. The Bete of Ivory Coast waste the considerable income obtained from the cultivation of cocoa and coffee on all kinds of ceremonial festivities.[56] One may talk of the necessity to stimulate the development of a backward country, but as long a dynamic spirit is lacking in the people, an increase in prosperity will remain wishful thinking. It is an enormous problem for the new African élite and the official leaders to develop a more dynamic cultural pattern and any hasty action during the development of large regions of Africa will only result in chaos. We ought not to be misled by the sight of some towns with a very modern character on the Western or Eastern coast or somewhere in Central Africa and think that they are characteristic of the stage of development of the whole of Central Africa. They are nothing more nor less than the small spots where Western influence and economic activity has created a centre of trade, mining, etc. The subsistence economies of Africa still dominate the economic pattern of the newly independent countries of Africa. Exploration and exploitation on a large scale of the natural resources of Africa have just been taken up. This continent possesses a considerable wealth of natural resources from raw materials up to and including all kinds of tropical agricultural products. However, most of Africa

55. H. T. Kimble, Tropical Africa I, Land and livelihood, New York 1960.
56. A. J. F. Köbben, The development of an underdeveloped territory, Sociologus NF VIII no. 1, p. 29.

158

is cut off, as much by lack of usable waterways, roads, railways and modern storage facilities, as by lack of education, knowledge and adequate techniques for meeting the requirements of distant markets. Aviation has opened up some areas but the capacity of airtransport is too small to have much influence on the development of this vast continent. To a very large extent Africa is cut off from the world economy. Only modern science and adequate economic, administrative but also political measures can in the long run possibly increase the development of Africa. There must be an end to the social and economic stagnation, which hampers even today the growth of Africa. Infrastructure has to be calculated as the primary need of Africa, but too many of the leaders of the new African states want to see at short notice, illuminating examples of economic and social development. The real nature of the revolt which is taking place in the minds and activities of the small African élite and which is demonstrated by the new economic and political demands, has to be seen as a revolt against the unchanged traditional structure of Africa. However, the African élite and the new governments too often blame the advanced countries for the very slow trend of African development. A transition of the African society to the stage in development of India or Brazil requires many decades, but the African élite is impatient. This results in very ambitious plans and projects which do not fit in well with the present rate of development. Most educated Africans are reaching out for a new state of affairs, i.e. participation in and links with the developed world, but also for an equal say in world politics. The membership of the new African nations of the United Nations and the right to record their vote and to discuss world problems creates a feeling of maturity. In so far as the African leaders fail to play an important role in the world economy and to fashion links with the modern world, political independence will prove to be a mirage. It will throw back their emergent peoples to economic misery and chaos. Disappointment will then throw them into the arms of Communism believing that they can have a firm hope in the great future, prosperity and development dangled before their eyes by the Communists on condition that they accept the Communist political system and technical assistance. However, they overlook that the mere wish to attain the economic benefits of a modern way of life does not supply also the means to achieve it. In their ambition to increase the trend of development they are sometimes so impatient, they fail to compare the benefits which may be expected from Western and Communist help. When the Western and especially the European countries stress sound development planning and the necessity of a large and extensive programme for technical

159

assistance, some African leaders look at such advice as a new form of colonialism. It is a good omen that the new African leaders are realizing more and more that they will gain most by co-operation with the Western countries. A look at figure XII shows the reciprocal economic interests between Western Europe and Africa. The capital investment policy of the colonial period pale into insignificance besides the present European aid and foreign private investment. The aid and technical assistance (public and private) to the underdeveloped and even backward African countries gives way to an economy of association—an association in freedom. The former colonial powers of Europe have the most qualified and experienced advisers to help to improve Africa's development. Neither the United Nations nor the U.S.A. or the Communists have at their disposal such experience and so many scientific institutes, familiar with the African problems and conditions. That is a good case for Euro-African co-operation. The very early stage of development can hardly prove beneficial, in spite of political independence, if a climate of political and economic security is not achieved and which will attract foreign private investment and technical assistance, besides multilateral or bilateral public aid. The barriers to economic development of Central Africa are to be found primarily in the field of infrastructure rather than in lack of human or natural. resources. Nothing will hamper the development of Africa more than the exertion of all kinds of multi -national organizations or of countries unfamiliar with the specific, complicated conditions of the African societies. The problems of Africa are completely different from those in other developing countries. In this connexion it should be borne in mind that the U.N. desire for compulsory unification of the Congo is nothing more nor less than frustrating a settled situation and creating chaos in an already vulnerable and unstable region. In the Congo a complex modern mining economy has been created besides considerable areas of specialized agricultural production, but it should be understood that Congo is in fact an artificially constructed political unit with many mutually hostile tribes, which have only one thing in common, viz. that they all belonged to the former Belgian colony. All efforts of the United Nations to settle this problem and to eliminate the hostile attitude between the various tribes at short notice will be doomed to failure, for history has proved that it will require decades. We only have to think of the hostile attitude between France and Germany which lasted for centuries before they decided to co-operate for their mutual benefit. In my opinion it is a fiction to think that we can talk of "the unity of the country" as long as tribes instead of political parties are the ruling native forces in Congo. It may sound well in U.N. or

American ears to work with and recognize Kasavubu as chief of state, but in fact he is only a puppet of the U.N. and as soon as the U.N. forces have left the Congo or their strength is reduced, the still strong and hostile tribes will take their chance. The theorists who want to apply a routine solution to the Congo and think that they will be able on the basis of such a system to create a modern African democratic state and a unified Congo, will be forced to recognize that the African traditional society can not be transformed overnight! The "big success" the U.N. have achieved in the Congo until now is a situation of simmering political tension, a decrease in prosperity and economic activity and also a retarding of the development of the regions which are poles apart and only tied by the artifical line of demarcation of the former Belgian colony. It is time that the development planners bear in mind that development diplomacy needs an approach based on reality.

Very instructive for our present world reformers is a passage in an article of Mair: "The new methods often involve harder work, the need for which is not fully understood, and the resentment which they provoke readily becomes associated with general resentment against colonial government, or with the specific grievance that African land has been alienated. One element in the appeal of Mau Mau was the promise of an end to soil conservation work; in the Union African leaders assert their right to ruin "our land" if they wish; in other places it is difficult to know how far refusal to do such work is primarily a form of political protest. One wonders how independent African leaders will deal with this situation".[57]

There was a lot of talking about a unification of the whole of Africa. However, it must be remembered that Pan-Africanism was originally an emotional protest by a small élite; it was not and is still not a practical plan for a United States of Africa as a political entity. The whole idea of Pan-Africanism was more an idea imported by ethic world reformers and not born in the mind of the big masses of African natives. The new African leaders and the élite are using this slogan as it is one of the principle means by which they are able to use this to obtain power. However, there are many African leaders with similar aspirations and that results more often in clashes and forming groups than in real unification. What is more, most Africans can not forget that the Arabs were the former slave-traders.

The African politician is mostly one of the few who received an education in an advanced country. To maintain himself the African

57. L. P. Mair, Social change in Africa. Internal affairs Vol. 36 no. 4. October 1960, p. 450.

politician has to play a dual role. His native followers are expecting much more than only political reform. They are in need of a new outlook upon life, which has to replace the lost social structure of tribal life. On the other hand he has to introduce new techniques and another attitude with regard to the duties of a human being in a developed economic society.

The African politician and the African political party have nothing in common with any other country in the world. The gap in development of thinking between the Dark Continent and the rest of the world is too wide and that stresses the need for a specific approach to African problems. Consequently, the attitude of some people to the situation in the Portuguese overseas provinces or in the Republic of South Africa is absolutely wrong, when they consider these problems in the same light as they would in the case of de-colonization of countries in Asia or Latin America. It is curious but also frightening, that many people who are too often not familiar with the existing conditions in those areas, pay a great deal of attention to the above mentioned parts of Africa, but do not say a word about the colonial way the U.S.S.R. is ruling the former developed countries of Eastern Europe such as Poland, Hungary and the Baltic states. I am not at all in favour of colonialism, but when there is a good chance for peaceful and constructive co-operation in the new developing countries between the former colonist or new settler and the native population, we should not hamper such a development of human relations. Now I would like to deal with the Portuguese provinces of Angola and Mozambique. It is regrettable that the U.N.-officials in Congo, responsible for the unification of Congo and advising the Central Congolese government, did not prevent the forming and training of a group of agitators in that country. The aim of this group of agitators, obtaining weapons in Congo, was to infiltrate Angola to create there unrest and chaos. First of all in my opinion the United Nations have neither the duty nor the right to support revolutionary forces within an area for which it has taken political responsibility. Second it proves an unfamiliarity with the realities of the constructive Portuguese policy in the overseas provinces. The attitude of Portugal to the coloured man has always been one of co-operation, but it is logical that you cannot treat an African native like a European, so long as the former is not able to look after himself. Relations between Portugal and a part of the Congo date from the fifteenth century. The following shows this: "Some of the earliest contacts read strangely today. The Portuguese in 1480-90 treated the King of the Congo, who was at once converted to Christianity, as a Christian kingly colleague; they accepted Congolese notables for education and as ambassadors to

162

the Court at Lisboa and instructed their own ambassadors to trea the Congo court with conventional respect.[58] Many parts of Africa are in turmoil, but the Portuguese try to create a community, wherein the white man and the negro can live together in peace and obtaining an increase in the standard of living. It is a continuation of the policy followed in the past. Portugal is a relatively small country, but it is doing everything for the development of the overseas provinces and the results are very often more striking than those in other places which have much foreign aid. It is remarkable that the U.S.A. are occupying themselves with Cuba, but disagree with the policy of Portugal to create a viable Euro-African society, to the benefit of all the members of this society. On the one side we hear in the United Nations and all over the world the slogan that we have to live peacefully together and that we have to strive for common ends, but on the other hand Portugal is blamed for its approach to the problem of co-operation of people of different colour and its succesful system of migration. Portugal is following its own policy and its claim is based not on expediency, but on what is considered to be valid on ethical and above all realistic motives. Already in 1606 the Portuguese laws are speaking of "the provinces and places overseas". The Constitution of 1822 proclaimed: "The Portuguese Nation is the union of all Portuguese in both hemispheres". In the same Constitution it is stressed: "We all wish no other term than the generous appellation of co-citizens of the same Country". In any family the young children and the parents form a unity, but it does not mean that the parents—having the heavy duty based on their experience and possessing the means therefore and giving guidance to the children to help them to grow to maturity—have no rights to decide to do what they think best".

The native people of the Portuguese provinces are not able to look after their own affairs. They still need a lot of assistance and their regions have to be developed. The free circulation of goods and the system of inter-regional payments within the Portuguese area is more benefiting to the people of the overseas provinces than the aid system to the other African states. I do not compare the value of a very progressive development policy of Portugal and the various confusing and very often illogical development programmes of the multi-national organizations. Some people like to blame Portugal for the fact that the standard of education in the overseas provinces

58. G. Hunter, The new societies of tropical Africa, London, 1962, p. 7 (Note: V. L. Cameron, Across Africa, London 1877, quoted by Ruth Slade in King Leopold's Congo, London, University Press for Institute of Race Relations 1962).

is still rather low and the income per capita is not too high, but if one is honest, one has to agree that many former colonial powers are more to blame. As well during the colonial period as during the time afterwards when technical assistance was given to the developing nations, these bigger countries had more means available to increase the number of coloured university-students. Also in some Southern States of the U.S.A. President Kennedy had to send police and military forces to safeguard the rights of all U.S. citizens—white or coloured people—to enter universities. It is the aim of Portugal to promote the agricultural and industrial development of all the overseas regions and above all the most backward of them. This transition requires time as in all the African nations. An enormous and impressive activity is building up the infrastructure. Public and private investment are going hand in hand to promote the economic progress in the overseas provinces. The integration of the Portuguese economy implies a freedom of circulation of goods and manpower and capital but also uniformity of the fiscal, social and economic policies to prevent the formation and maintenance of artificial distinctions. It is interesting that Kimble wrote about the co-operation between the Portuguese and the African in the overseas provinces: "The average Portuguese farmer in tropical Africa has not the least objection to labouring with his own hands or for that matter, doing everything himself. The average Belgian or British settler, on the other hand, automatically assumes that Africans will do most of the manual work for him".[59] In view of the restrictions on the imports of products of developing countries and the fall of prices for commodities on the world market, the overseas provinces of Portugal are in this respect in a privileged position as a result of the integrated economy.

The widening of the home market which will result from the fusion of the Portuguese regions which enjoy customs autonomy will allow the market mechanisms to function freely and equally on all national territory. We must not overlook that Portugal as our N.A.T.O. ally has to be supported in order to maintain or promote the prosperity. Only a healthy Portuguese economy is able to meet the military commitments as set by N.A.T.O. and to go on with the intensive development programme to the benefit of the overseas provinces. When we consider the eagerness of many African nations to be associated with the European common market, we see that the Portuguese overseas provinces are already profiting by integration with an advanced country, which the new African nations

59. H. T. Kimble, Tropical Africa I, Land and Livelihood, p. 591, New York 1960.

still have to wait for. The Portuguese policy of assimilation should be understood in terms of the creation of a will to live together and not as a policy directed to interrupt the development of the native coloured population of the overseas provinces. There is every reason to give a fair chance to the Portuguese policy of developing Angola and Mozambique, although it is different from the generally accepted pattern. The development programmes are not only sound but also very ambitious and that must be counted as a benefit to the African provinces. Many new African nations are right to be jealous about this development and policy, but it does not give them the right to hamper this development and especially not when they themselves are unable to attain comparable economic progress and political stability.

I am paying so much attention to Angola and Mozambique, as in my opinion there is such misunderstanding, that I am justified in providing another view of this affair. Remarks are made in connexion with the policy of the "assimilado". The "assimilado" is the African who has attained the status of a full Portuguese citizen by adopting European culture and abandoning his native customs, by being able to use the Portuguese language, by possessing some trade or profession and by completing his military service. We mentioned above the necessity to create a new outlook upon life, the creation of an adequate infrastructure and a selfsustaining economy in the new African states, but pointed as well to the lack of a common native language. The native man in Angola and Mozambique is placed by the Portuguese development policy in a much more privileged position. The Portuguese are striving for assimilation. Once an African has become an assimilado, he becomes a tax-payer and that is the main reason why the number of assimilados is still rather small. I have mentioned already above how migration in the Portuguese provinces became a reality and that discrimination is not a characteristic of the Portuguese society neither in the homeland nor in the overseas provinces!

I would like to point at what is written in "The British Survey" of May 1962 about Portugal in Africa on page 15: "Who are 'the Angolan leaders'? If there existed any prospects of a genuine negro government formed by persons manifestly enjoying mass support throughout the territory and having such competence in political and economic management as have the majority of those who have come to the fore in the independent French-speaking states of Africa, for instance, or in Nigeria, there would be so strong a case for the transfer of powers, that no Portuguese Government could resist it in the existing climate of opinion. We, for our part, should be the first to recommend it. But it is sheer dishonesty to pretend that any such situation exists". My support for the Portuguese development policy and political structure of the Portuguese society is based upon the fact that co-operation between the people of the free world and succesful migration is often a better solution than widening the gap between the coloured people and the white men.

There are not many countries in the world, that are peopled entirely by only one racial stock. On the contrary most countries are more or less multi-racial. Where the peoples of different racial origins, cultural backgrounds and even different educational level live together and form a political entity, development possibilities increase. Such a situation we meet in India and in many countries of Latin America. The basic principles of a multi-racial society are the existence of a healthy mixture of the various racial elements, the lack of fear or suspicion and a loyal distribution of political power. In the stage of development the white minority or the race with the highest education will have to give guidance in such a society until a complete distribution of political power can be achieved. This has nothing to do with discrimination. The main purpose is only that the most capable people are guiding the whole country to political and economic maturity. Nobody can deny that in each society, advanced or backward, social promotion has to rest on a solid basis so that the responsibilities assigned correspond to the capacity to carry them out. Very often the race or group with a much higher level of education and experience will form a minority. This is the case in many developing countries with a white minority. As a result of the colonial period there exists much suspicion against the white minority by the coloured people. It is true, that too often the white minority did not understand the evolution which has taken place, thereby creating suspicion and tension, which could have been prevented by a more progressive and understanding attitude. Important is also the fact that the white minority was outnumbered in course of time by coloured people originating from elsewhere and by a considerable increase in population of that group. It resulted in a struggle between the white and the coloured people. Very often the white minority, being numerically small and at the same time the most prosperous people, rejected the concept of majority rule. This is the case in the Republic of South Africa and has resulted in the "apartheid". In the Portuguese overseas provinces we are meeting an evolution and it is there that we observe a positive policy to achieve equality of individuals regardless of race, resulting in course of time to majority rule within that mixed-racial community. This is a sophisticated policy of gradual racial integration. Africans,

166

schooled in Western countries and familiar with the principles of democracy, are fervently in favour of equality of individuals and majority rule. However, and it is regrettable that they like to apply these ideas straight away to all Africans and sometimes also to the Asiatics settled in Africa, but not to the white minority. The result is tension between the white and the Africans.

In my opinion the white has also a certain right to stay on living where he has built up a new white prosperous community. The whites spent part of their lives or even their whole life in Africa and played an important role in the development of the backward country, which has been unquestionably an advantage to the native population. It should not be forgotten that there are white settlers whose families have been in Africa for many generations and for whom that African country became their fatherland, meaning more to them than their former European country. This is especially the case in the Republic of South Africa, where the Afrikaners have built up a new nation with only very loose ties with Great Britain and historic ties with the Netherlands. In the Republic of South Africa it is obligatory for the natives to possess a pass and these are checked. This measure was taken to prevent too many Africans coming into the country in order to find a job there and to earn more money. Each government has to prevent unemployment and has for that reason to refuse the inflow of too many people. The inflow of Africans was difficult to prevent as because of the geographical conditions and only by pass control could the illegal newcomers be found and sent back. There is no nation in the world allowing free entry to everybody who likes to settle there for ever. Even tourists have to show their passports! Where foreigners are allowed to work in a country, it does not mean they must necessarily have the same rights as the people of that country. In the Netherlands many Spanish and Italian labourers are working. They receive the same pay and have all equal social securities as the Dutch labourer. However, he is not allowed to vote for the election of members of parliament. In the Republic of South Africa we have a comparable state of affairs. There is a large white community which has developed very succesfully that part of Africa into one of the most advanced regions of Africa. The native Africans and for a long time also coloured newcomers received the benefits of this white settlement. In comparison with the living conditions in other parts of Africa, the Negroes earned more money to live on, However, the policy of the government was not in favour of mixture of races and unquestionably there was and still is a distinct race-discrimination. This policy was reinforced when African nationalism became a real threat to the white minority in the Republic of South

167

Figure XIV

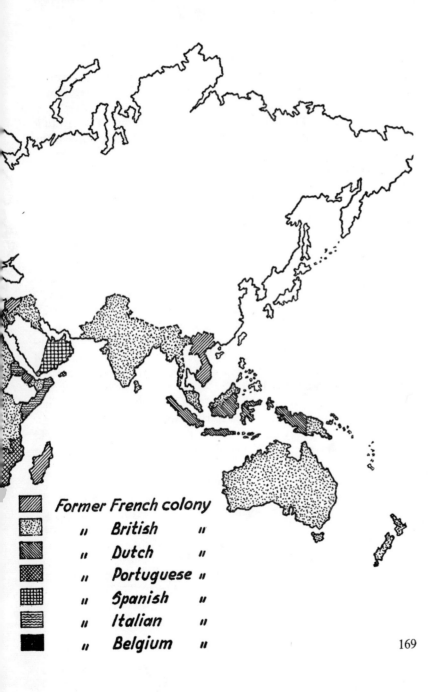

EUROPEAN COLONIES
IN THE PAST

Former French colony
       "   British   "
       "   Dutch   "
       "   Portuguese "
       "   Spanish   "
       "   Italian   "
       "   Belgium   "

Africa. There was no talk at all of the creation of a multi-racial society. Although in my opinion a white minority has a right to stay where it settled down a long time ago (therefore the Afrikaners can not and should not be blamed when they fight for their existence in the Republic of South Africa) they will have to accept the realities of the moment. It means that the acceptance of an increase of the distribution of political power and an end to racial discrimination is a necessity. Maintaining "apartheid" can only result in increased tension. The argument that the white created the prosperity of South Africa and the coloured people therefore have no political rights, is now thoroughly rejected by the new African nations. This attitude of the white minority is inviting serious trouble. All measures taken at the moment by the government will not satisfy African nationalist feeling. The Republic of South Africa is creating the Transkei as the new country of the Bantu. When the coloured men wish to stay and to work in the Republic of South Africa, there are no objections but they have to respect the political power of the white society and to accept "apartheid". I believe that the time has come that at least the coloured élite in the Republic should have equal rights. The argument that the African is still not ready for freedom is in conflict with the policy of the South African government in creating a separate and independent Bantu society in Transkei. I am strongly in favour of the principle that a white society, established in Africa for centuries must not be eliminated, but a change in attitude to the sense of the Portuguese migration will be a condition for the continuation of the existence of the Republic of South Africa. Marchand writes: "The white man's burden—in those few places where the white man still has the will to bear it—should be facilitated by the West, instead of knocked off his shoulder".[60] However, the white minority then has to understand the spirit of the times and act accordingly, instead of cultivating an out of date policy. This may sound unpleasant to the white people of the Republic of South Africa, but there is no sense in neglecting reality and the present situation in Africa! The decade of rising expectations will coincide with the desire for political and social equality for all, regardless of the colour of their skin and for that reason to secure a white settlement in Africa, the South Africans will have to consider their present policy. Co-operation will have to replace "apartheid", but that does not mean neglecting the historical rights of the white colonists. Education of the coloured people of South Africa on a large scale will facilitate a transition to more acceptable forms of political structure in this

60. J. Marchand, The two native Africa's. General Military Review, June 1962.

Republic, giving the coloured people a fair share in the ruling of the country.

The Republic of South Africa can be won for the West in the future, but it will be necessary to pay a just price.

It would be wrong to neglect the constructive powers which are existing in Africa. In spite of an avowed policy of neutralism and the abhorrence of "neo-colonialism", many African states seek co-operation with the former colonial power. Therefore many "British" and "French" African nations have maintained good relationships respectively with Great Britain and France. The latter continues to play a leading role in aiding the economic development of their former colonies. Even African countries not associated with Great Britain or France, respectively in the British Commonwealth or the French Communauté, are receiving aid and technical assistance. The slogan of "Aid without strings" is not always respected. On the contrary many new African nations return to the former colonial European power in order to increase the amount of aid and to benefit from the experience and knowledge of the former dominating power. Especially those new nations of Africa, governed by highly qualified statesmen, mostly experienced in British or French politics, are realizing that they will gain more by co-operation with the European advanced countries than by cultivating an extreme nationalism and neutralism. The political ambitions of some African nations and the territorial ambitions of others are hampering the achievement of unification of Africa and the result is that we are still left with so many African states. Some of them are very small in size as well as in the number of people and in such cases economic development is really a great problem. Gabon for example has only 400.000 people.

After all, Africa south of the Sahara is a part of the world where we have to face a large number of problems of all kinds and for that reason the development of that part of the Dark Continent is a very difficult and complicated affair.

North Africa has problems of another kind. The Greeks and the Romans had a great influence in the past, but it was eliminated by the militant Mohammedan religion carried on by the Arabs through Egypt and North Africa, thereby introducing the Moslem faith. The present state of affairs in Africa north of the Sahara shows the influence of the main European industrial countries of the nineteenth and early twentieth centuries. Italy and Germany were eliminated from the colonial world as a result of the two World Wars.

I will not describe the various countries of Africa around the Mediterranean. Egypt, Ethiopia, Sudan, Libya, Tunisia, Algeria and Morocco have all obtained independence. Politically Egypt has the most dynamic influence on the affairs in Africa, but the economic problems it has to face are enormous. Particularly the economic development is difficult through a lack of sufficient natural resources and arable land. Ethiopia has the longest history of real independent status in the whole of Africa and a much better chance for prosperity, but its geographically isolated location (it is surrounded by mountains) and the archaic political structure are hampering progress.

Libya, the result of welding three separate countries into one, has today the benefit of the export of oil, but its million nomadic Bedouins are a real problem as they have a long way to go before they emerge into the modern world. One of the many reasons why this country makes slow progress towards national unity is that there are such poor communications between the three provinces. There are only about a few hundred miles of railway! Libya appears to have a bright commercial future from oil. Investment by the oil companies amounted to £55 million in 1960. The exploitation of the oil wells led to the location of more than 500 water wells to the benefit of the small farmers and the cattle-breeding nomads. Ethiopia and Libya are following a policy which attracts foreign private investment to the benefit of their economic development. The Sudanese development is retarded by the fact that here the southern primitive pagans and the northern Moslems, the latter strongly influenced by Egypt, have to co-operate. The Negroes in the south are hence striving for independence from the north. This combined with the lack of an adequate infrastructure and of sufficient natural resources, does not give much hope for a short-term economic development. Tunisia is facing many economic problems. The high birth-rate and the large number of French residents who left the country following independence have created unemployment and there is not enough capital available for the realization of the development plans. The available wealth in minerals is satisfactory, but the interest of foreign private enterprise to exploit these riches is very unsatisfactory. Socially and economically the country is progressing. Many of the Tunisians have the same standard of living as the Europeans, but the nomads on the contrary are mostly illiterate and lead an extremely precarious existence.

The economic value of Morocco is largely derived from minerals. Foreign private investment in the mining activity is not too satisfactory, but its wealth of minerals opens up possibilities for future economic development.

Generally speaking all the countries mentioned have a tremendous task in destroying illiteracy and raising the standard of living. Po-

172

litical influences are hampering in many of them a more rapid economic development although some of these countries have considerable natural resources. From an economic point of view all these countries have not until now been of very much importance, with the exception of Libya and Algeria, both possessing large oil reserves. However, from a strategic point of view they are very important. Behind them are located the enormous natural resources of tropical Africa. If the Communists could manage to attract one of them within their political camp, the position of N.A.T.O. in the Mediterranean would become hopeless. For that reason aid and technical assistance, and the stimulation of foreign private investment are of the highest importance in order to develop these countries and to increase their prosperity. Both infrastructure and education require all our attention. We can not take the risk of letting them fall into the hands of the U.S.S.R. The internal political structure and the large existing élite will facilitate the development of these countries. The promotion of better relations between the countries of this area of Africa and the West must be our main target. Once co-operation on a large scale is made possible, economic development programmes will be very promising.

As we have seen, the development of Africa is not at all an easy affair, notwithstanding the presence of considerable human and natural resources. Africa has many specific problems, not comparable with those in the other developing areas. Lack of an adequate infrastructure, problems originating from the primitive society (tribes and traditions) and the too ambitious or over-sensitive attitude of many African leaders, will have a retarding influence on the development of the Dark Continent. Assistance of the West is indispensable! Great care must be taken to show Africans that Western aid and technical assistance does not mean perpetuation of European political influence. They must be free to make their own economic decisions and they will start to realize that they will have all the benefit of agreements freely reached.

Most African trade is with Europe. As we have seen, Europe has for economic and strategic reasons a sincere interest in the course of events in Africa. It should never be overlooked that Europe has most experience and knowledge of the conditions of Africa, but also in many other parts of the underdeveloped world. The Europeans are familiar with all the problems resulting from tradition, illiteracy and low levels of education, tropical diseases, social structures and so on. A look at Figure XIV shows all the former European colonies. For that reason the experience of Europe must be used to the largest extent for the development of the new countries. The still existing links or the restoration of these links between developing countries and Europe should not be interrupted by nonsensical ideas, propagating that aid and technical assistance shall be given by preference through multi-national organizations or countries which have never owned colonies. The latter are lacking to a certain extent the required experience and the examples we present are proof of that. By the inefficiency of the multi-national organizations huge sums of capital are wasted and could be spent more efficiently, while the selection of technical advisers leaves much to be desired. A summing-up of the number of the most important existing institutes in the field of technical aid in Europe is presented in chapter IX (p. 183). I can not see any honest or reasonable argument why European bilateral aid and technical assistance should be inferior to that of the United States of America as long as independence of the receiving developing countries is fully respected. We are in the free world striving for equality, elimination of racial discrimination and above all for co-operation. The discrimination of European multilateral or bilateral aid by many people of the United Nations may be founded on the fear that European aid is given only for sound development plans and programmes and because only really qualified and experienced people are used for technical assistance. Europe has an age-long experience in world political affairs such as no other advanced nation possesses and Europe has also every interest in co-operating freely with the developing countries. European private investors have also an age-long experience in the foundation of private enterprises in underdeveloped countries and still have at their disposal experienced people, familiar with conditions in less-developed societies. The European countries have just as great a need to prevent unemployment as all nations and have for that reason sometimes a distinct preference for tied bilateral grants or loans. Altruïsm has its limits!

The European N.A.T.O. countries have a great stake in the development of the Middle Eastern countries and Africa not only for economic reasons but also on political and strategic grounds. Political stability and the existence of non Communist independent nations in this part of the world are of high value. As the U.S.A. who did not like or accept Communist influence in the Western hemisphere, Europe has a distinct preference for a rapid growth to political maturity and prosperity in freedom in Africa, the Middle East and Asia. Prosperity in the developing free world may prevent the expansion of Communist influence. Economic co-operation with the developing countries is to the benefit of the latter and of the West. As I showed the aid to the developing free world is not an easy affair

174

and will take time but it is a necessary prerequisite if we want to create world wide prosperity and political stability.

Summing up we may say that what we have to achieve in the developing countries is:

a. Elimination of illiteracy and education in order to create a qualified élite,

b. A rapid increase of income per capita,

c. A rapid reduction of inequalities in income distribution,

d. A relatively stable price level and an equilibrium in the balance of payments,

e. The avoidance of marked disparity in the prosperity and economic growth of different countries and areas,

f. A diversification of the manufactured goods and farm products.

There will be conflicts between these objectives. It may be that the development of population will require priority for the exension of employment possibilities, while elsewhere reduction of inequalities in income distribution is more important in order to prevent a social revolution.

Western aid has only a peace preserving character and that is the indirect interest which is linking N.A.T.O. with the whole complex of development activities. It is a very important indirect interest and it is for this reason that I had to present a very general description of the developing world and the problems we will meet in the performance of this great task. However, it was also important to show that white minorities in the developing countries have their rights and need an understanding of their specific position, but also that the creation of a multi-racial Euro-African community can be a solution which commands respect; when it gives a fair distribution of political power without race discrimination.

The noted historian Toynbee wrote: "Immigrant ruling minorities whose retreat has been cut off feel that they have their backs to the wall. They are faced with a painful choice. Either they must resign themselves to the prospect that sooner or later, they will have to accept the status of an unprivileged minority among a majority whom they now feel to be inferior to them culturally, or they must try to hold on to their present supremacy by main force against a rising tide of revolt against their domination. The second course would obviously be fatal for the minority; for, even its belief in its own present cultural superiority is justified, numbers will tell in the long run, considering that culture is contagious and that an ascendency based on cultural superiority is therefore a wasting asset. On the other hand, voluntary abdication in favour of a majority whom one feels to be one's inferiors is a very hard alternative for human pride

175

to accept". [61] Furthermore he points to the fact that really serious trouble arises where the dominant foreigners are not "pilgrims and sejourners" but are permanent settlers. The problem of the white minorities and the creation of multi-racial communities have a not inconsiderable influence on the Western development diplomacy!

There are many roads leading to Rome and likewise there are many ways to bring prosperity to the people of developing regions. Co-operation with the underdeveloped people in any form is what we are striving for and one country will try to achieve this by the creation of a multi-racial society and another by giving aid to the new independent nation which was his former colony, while the non-colonial countries do not have a specific interest in the development of selected new nations. Most important is that the people of the developing regions shall obtain prosperity and equal rights regardless of the colour of their skin!

61. A. Toynbee, History's warning to Africa, Optima, June 1959, p. 55.

CHAPTER IX

THE ORGANIZATIONAL STRUCTURE FOR AID
AND TECHNICAL ASSISTANCE

As mentioned in the preceding chapters the West is giving aid not only on human and ethical grounds but also on economic, political and strategic grounds. The latter three motives are the most important for our prosperity and defence. The cold war between East and West as a result of the Communist threat is forcing us to prevent as much as possible the U.S.S.R. gaining influence in the free world and especially in the underdeveloped world. A study of the most suitable organization for Western aid and technical assistance has to take this fact into account and it was for this reason that I have already pointed out the danger of the Communists abusing in the United Nations organizations for aid in order to infiltrate into those underdeveloped countries and areas where they hope and expect to gain political influence. No doubt, it would be preferable on ethical grounds if the sole motive of policy with respect to the developing countries, which are for the majority uncommitted in the cold war, was a desire by the advanced countries to help the "have-nots". Yet, and this may be regrettable, in the present time of cold war, analysis of political action must be founded on realities, not on wishful thinking or on delusions. This state of affairs is not as unfortunate as might at first appear, because it is not inconceivable that the developing countries receive even more aid and technical assistance than they would have got if there were no controversy between East and West. In our attempt to persuade the uncommitted countries not to give themselves to our main opponent, the West is spending much money on the various aid programmes. The amount of Western aid to the developing world is many times higher than that of the U.S.S.R. and Communist China and, what is more, the latter give their aid principally to selected countries where they think they will achieve their political ends best. To channel Western aid through the United Nations organizations would mean that there is a possibility that Communists are sent out for technical assistance and charged with the realization of certain projects under the flag of the United Nations. In figure XV we give a survey of all the organizations dealing with aid and technical assistance and this shows among others the widespread fields of activity of the United Nations, wherein the Communists can infiltrate and especially in those countries not receiving bilateral Communist aid.

In the interest of the West I would prefer to channel most of our multilateral aid and technical assistance through multi-national organizations of which the Communist countries do not form a part. It does not mean that I would advice the elimination of the U.N. completely with regard to all aid activities. However, I would like to limit the U.N. activities to assistance in cases of pestilence such as famine, earthquakes, epidemics and so forth. In all these cases the assistance has a temporary but also a charitable character.

In this respect there is an enormous task ahead of us. The famine in many parts of the underdeveloped world is dreadful and baffles description. It is a shame that the prosperous nations, sometimes having at their disposal enormous quantities of surplus foodstuffs, have done so little to combat famine rigorously. One only has to read the book of J. de Castro and to look at the pictures in it, to feel awfully ashamed that living conditions as described in this book exist in our present world.[62] Instead of occupying itself with all kinds of sometimes poorly co-ordinated programmes and wasting large amounts of money, the United Nations should organize a world-wide campaign to put an end in the shortest time to famine! I should really be surprised if the U.S.S.R. would pay its reasonable share of such a campaign. However, even without Soviet participation the West is able to accomplish here a great task and relatively not requiring such a large amount of money. Such a Western campaign, using the channels of the United Nations would create an enormous goodwill, although that must not be our aim. It is our sacred duty!

In my opinion there is no objection to United Nation activities in the field of promotion of interregional economic co-operation or integration. In this respect the Economic Commission for Latin America (E.C.L.A.), the Economic Commission for Africa (E.C.A.) and the Economic Commission for Asia and the Far East (E.C.A.F.E.) have done and are still doing a good job. Furthermore I could mention the I.C.A.O., the F.A.O. and so on. In these activities the Communists have not the opportunity to settle down in a developing country and to influence the internal political affairs under the flag of the U.N.

It is not at all my intention to eliminate the influence of the developing nations in the organizations charged with multi-national aid and technical assistance programmes. On the contrary I would like

62. J. de Castro, Le livre noir de la faim, Paris 1961.

to enlist them on a much larger scale, as will be shown later, but not only within the framework of the United Nations. It is not my intention to commit the developing countries to a certain country or alliance endangering their chance to maintain neutrality. As a world forum the United Nations are of high value, especially if the nations regard the problems submitted to them, objectively and respect international law.

Before I explain my views of the organization of Western aid and technical assistance, I shall point out that there are already numerous regional organizations for facilitating development by their own means and co-operation.

In many regional organizations the main aim is co-operation in the economic field. However, the developing countries must realize that co-operation will not be sufficient. As in Europe where advanced countries have established the European Common Market, which may soon be extended to more members, the developing nations have to strive for economic integration. With their weak economies it is the only way to accelerate economic progress. The integration of the economies, and of the social and economic policies of the countries concerned, with all the political implications that this involves, will be necessary not only to obtain a stronger competing position in the world market, but also to widen the regional market. Figure XVI presents a survey of existing economic integration between the developing countries. The ambitions of the leaders of some nations and the political implications of economic integration will hamper the creation of common markets.

There is the Latin American Free Trade Association (L.A.F.T.A.) promoting its own version of a common market agreement. Basically, the seven L.A.F.T.A. nations have agreed to a rather loose association to eliminate over a 12-year period barriers against trade in products now being traded. This organization provides a framework for negotiation and discussion of economic and trade problems. Its operations would serve to broaden the area of mutual economic interest and co-operation. It is important that the nations involved are beginning to recognize that their economic problems transcend national boundaries. It is to be hoped that the L.A.F.T.A. will be expanded with more Latin American countries. There exists also a Central American Common Market. The regional integration plans for Latin America, as set forth in the Latin American Free Trade Association and the Central American Treaty for Economic Integration, will enable the Latin American countries to expand their markets reciprocally, thus creating one of the basic elements for future development.

Today the principle of the indivisibility of prosperity and economic

N.A.T.O. COUNTRIES-MEMBERSHIP OF (x) OR RELATIONS

ECONOMIC AND TECHNICAL ASS

Commissions, Institutions and Funds	U.S.A.	U.K.	France	Canada	Netherlands	Belgiu
1. *United Nations*	x	x	x	x	x	x
E.C.O.S.O.C.	x	x	o	o	o	o
E.C.A.	o	o	o	o	o	o
E.C.A.F.E.	o	o	o	o	o	o
E.C.L.A.	o	o	o	o	o	o
T.A.B.	o	o	o	o	o	o
T.A.C.	o	o	o	o	o	o
F.A.O.	x	x	x	x	x	x
I.A.E.A.	x	x	x	x	x	x
I.B.R.D.	x	x	x	x	x	x
I.C.A.O.	x	x	x	x	x	x
I.D.A.	x	x	x	x	x	x
I.F.C.	x	x	x	x	x	x
I.L.O.	x	x	x	x	x	x
I.T.U.	x	x	x	x	x	x
U.N. Special Fund	x	x	x	x	x	o
U.N.E.S.C.O.	x	x	x	x	x	x
U.N.I.C.E.F.	x	x	x	x	x	x
U.N.R.W.A.	o	o	o	o	o	o
U.N.T.A.A.	o	o	o	o	o	o
2. *European Economic Community*						
Development Fund			x		x	x
3. *Organization for Economic Co-operation and Development*	x	x	x	x	x	x
Development Assistance Committee	o	o	o	o	o	o
Technical Assistance Committee	o	o	o	o	o	o
4. *Colomboplan*	x	x		x		
5. *Commission for Technical Co-operation in Africa South of the Sahara*		x	x			x

Figure XV

Luxem-bourg	Norway	Denmark	Italy	Iceland	Portugal	Western Germany	Greece	Turkey
x	x	x	x	x	x		x	x
o	o	x	o	o	o		o	o
o	o	o	o	o	o		o	o
o	o	o	o	o	o		o	o
o	o	o	o	o	o		o	o
o	o	o	o	o	o	o	o	o
o	o	o	o	o	o		o	o
x	x	x	x	x	x	x	x	x
x	x	x	x	x	x	x	x	x
x	x	x	x	x		x	x	x
x	x	x	x	x	x	x	x	x
x	x	x	x	x		x	x	x
x	x	x	x	x		x	x	x
x	x	x	x	x	x	x	x	x
x	x	x	x	x	x	x	x	x
o	o	x	x	o	o		o	o
x	x	x	x			x	x	x
x	x	x	x	x	x	x	x	x
o	o	o	o	o	o		o	o
o	o	o	o	o	o		o	o
x			x			x		
x	x	x	x	x	x	x	x	x
o	o	o	o	o	o	o	o	o
o	o	o	o	o	o	o	o	o
					x			

as well as social progress of all nations has been fully accepted. It creates new sources of co-operation between the more advanced countries and the newly developing regions. President Kennedy's Alliance for Progress programme and the Charter of Punta del Este will promote the development of Latin America.

In connexion with Asia I refer to the Colombo Plan. The Colombo Plan is the name given to the sum of the co-operative effort which the countries of South and South East Asia, helped by member countries outside the region (U.K., Australia, Canada, Japan, U.S.A. and New Zealand), are making to develop their economies and raise the living standards of their people. Most of the development programmes of the member countries in the region are financed domestically. These countries also help one another with technical assistance and some capital development funds. Member countries outside the area offer aid in the form of outright grants, inter-governmental loans, loans by public banks and various kinds of private grants and investments. Here we see a co-operation which will stimulate economic progress both by personal effort and outside aid. Political unrest inside the region is hampering too often a smooth and increasing development. Another promising organization is the Association of South-East Asia (Thailand, Philippines and Malaya), which promotes close economic co-operation and in certain fields integration. The U.S.A. is very eager to stimulate foreign private investment within their region. Furthermore I have to mention the Aid India Club, established to accelerate the development by aid from a number of Western countries.

The original institutions of the French Community have fallen into disuse; some of the original members, such as Gabon, still claim to belong, and others like Cameroun, never joined. French aid and support continue none the less, on a bilateral basis and as the amount of French aid is enormous and still increasing, relations with the former metropolitan power are as good as they could be. France is paying all attention to rapid increased development of its former colonies and has made available a high amount from public funds for this purpose.

The Organization for Economic Co-operation and Development (O.E.C.D.) proceeded from the Organization for European Economic Co-Operation (O.E.E.C.), is aiming among others at a contribution to sound economic expansion in member as well as non-member countries in the process of economic development and at the expansion of world trade on a multilateral, non-discriminatory basis in accordance with international obligations. It is very important that it has been determined to pursue the purpose of this organization in a manner consistent with their obligations in other international organizations or institutions in which the members participate or under agreements to which they are a party. It opens a possibility for the developing countries associated with members of the O.E.C.D. to benefit from this organization. Not only the developing countries of the British Commonwealth and the French Communauté, but also the other Asiatic, Latin American and African countries will be involved in the development plans and programmes of the O.E.C.D. The Development Assistance Committee of the O.E.C.D. (D.A.C.) will be fully engaged in studies and consultations which will be essential to the performance of technical assistance. Experiences in the field of technical assistance will also be exchanged.

The European Economic Community (Common Market) is also dealing with aid and technical assistance to the associated overseas countries. The purpose of the European Development Fund of the E.E.C. will be to promote the economic and social development of the overseas countries and territories and to establish close economic relations between them and the Community as a whole. The aim is to confirm the solidarity which binds Europe and overseas countries and to ensure the development of their prosperity, in accordance with the Charter of the United Nations and furthermore the task is "the association of overseas countries and territories with the Community in order to increase trade and pursuing jointly their effort towards economic and social development".

The association with the E.E.C. not only offers the overseas countries many of the benefits of the Common Market, it also gives them extra advantages which take account of their special needs. The importance of this association is shown by the fact that the European Community imported more than 60% of the exports of the associated overseas countries.

Although a great many more organizations could be mentioned, which are essential to the developing countries, I will leave it at that but I would like to make an exception for the situation in this respect in Europe. The number of existing institutions in important European N.A.T.O. countries, occupied with expert training and with research in the field of technical aid to developing countries (according to unpublished E.E.C. sources) are:

Countries	Belgium	Neth.	France	Italy	W. Germ.	U.K.
Number of institutions	36	14	68	13	31	n.a.*

* In the U.K. expert training and research is principally in hands of the universities and institutes.

GENERAL CENTRAL AMERICAN
AGREEMENT FOR ECONOMIC
INTEGRATION

GUATEMALA
HONDURAS
EL SALVADOR
NICARAGUA
COSTA RICA

LATIN AMERICA FREE
TRADE ASSOCIATION (L.A.F.T.A.)

MEXICO
COLOMBIA
ECUADOR
PERU
BRAZIL
PARAGUAY
ARGENTINA
URUGUAY
CHILE

MONROVIA COUNTRIES

UNION AFRICAINE
ET MALGACHE

MAURITANIA
NIGER
CHAD
SENEGAL
UPPER VOLTA
IVORY COAST
DAHOMEY
CAMEROONS
C.A.R.
GABON
MIDDLE CONGO
MALAGASY RE

SIERRA LEO
LIBERIA
SOMALILAN
ETHIOPIA
NIGERIA
TOGOLAND
LIBYA
TUNISIA

Figure

184

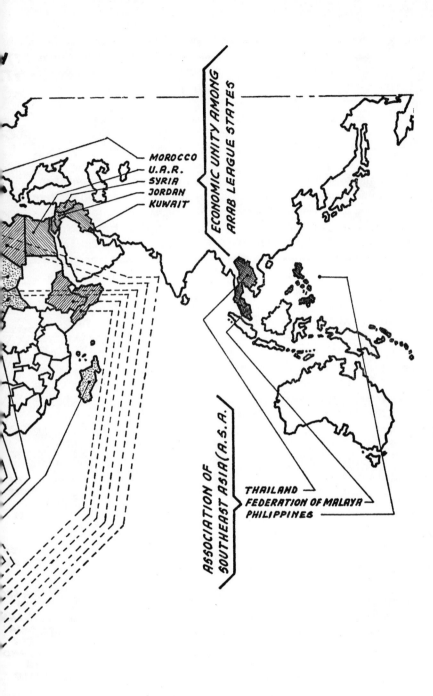

MOROCCO
U.A.R.
SYRIA
JORDAN
KUWAIT

ECONOMIC UNITY AMONG ARAB LEAGUE STATES

ASSOCIATION OF SOUTHEAST ASIA (A.S.A.

THAILAND
FEDERATION OF MALAYA
PHILIPPINES

The purpose of the summing up is to show how many organizations are dealing with aid and technical assistance to the developing countries. On top of this, large numbers approach the national organizations dealing with bilateral aid and technical assistance.

It will not be surprising that there is too little co-ordination, in spite of a certain exchange of information concerning aid, foreign private investment and technical assistance. The various development programmes are not co-ordinated and this results in a considerable waste of effort and capital. There is every reason for a revision of the system of aid and technical assistance that we are using at the moment. As I mentioned above, I have a decided preference for keeping all Western developing activities outside each multi-national organization, of which the Communists form part and in consequence the United Nations have to be ruled out, except for the humane activities mentioned above.

The United Nations Charter recognizes the need for regional groupings. The nations constituting the O.E.C.D. by reason of their historical and cultural connexions and, most important, by reason of their importance to the world economy have declared their joint determination to assume their full responsibilities in view of the enormous problems of world economic growth and balance. The O.E.C.D. is an organization which is not linked with N.A.T.O. All countries of the free world are able to co-operate within the framework of the O.E.C.D., without being committed to N.A.T.O. or linked with the East-West controversy.

In the Western world there are two multi-national organizations, dealing with the development activities as mentioned, the O.E.C.D. (D.A.C.) and the E.E.C. (European Development Fund). The O.E.C.D. has a worldwide character, while the E.E.C. is covering a more limited area. Even if the United Kingdom and other European countries should join the E.E.C., the area covered by this organization would be much smaller than that of the O.E.C.D. The logical conclusion would be that preference should be given to the O.E.C.D. However, as I have tried to explain above, the links between the European countries and the overseas developing countries and territories, based on historical grounds and so far maintained very often by reciprocal agreement, are still very tight. This is to a large extent owing to the benefits the overseas countries obtain by this co-operation. One may wonder that I have not mentioned N.A.T.O. as an employable organization. Most of the developing countries do not like to commit themselves in any form to one of the opposing blocs. They do not want to get involved in a world war, although some skilful leaders have succeeded in extracting advantages by taking aid wherever and whenever it has been offered without falling into any political pitfall.

186

The risks they accept are appealing, especially in view of the economic dependency as a result of tied Soviet aid, linked with the obligation to accept technical assistance for the realization of a certain project or programme. Anyhow, I would never suggest to use the N.A.T.O. for any development activity for the uncommitted countries, in order to prevent any idea of neo-colonialism. Our main aim with the development diplomacy is to create economic and political co-operation in complete freedom, thereby eliminating any idea of a direct link between N.A.T.O. and any developing country. It will also prevent political pressure on them by the U.S.S.R. on account of being linked with N.A.T.O.

As the E.E.C. Development Fund is covering a smaller area than the D.A.C. of the O.E.C.D., but also fewer Western countries are members of the E.E.C., the ideal solution could be to concentrate all Western development activities in the O.E.C.D. However, there is a proverb "don't throw old shoes away before you have new ones", and in this case I would not suggest the ruling out of the E.E.C. Development Fund. On the contrary, there are firm grounds to use both for the present. When Great Britain and other European countries have become members, the area covered by the E.E.C. Development Fund is extended. The combined experience and knowledge besides the large number of scientific institutions and research centres as well as the existing ties of co-operation between Europe and the overseas developing countries, shows strongly in favour of an undisturbed growth of the E.E.C. Development Fund. However, this does not mean that there should not be very close co-operation between these two Western organizations. Likewise a reorganization within these two bodies will be required.

The task of the D.A.C. is to review periodically together both the amount and the nature of the contributions of the O.E.C.D. members to aid programmes and to make a study of the principles on which governments might equitably determine their respective contributions to the common aid effort and the various means of encouraging the flow of private capital, such as through fiscal incentives, multilateral conventions for the protection of private property and multilateral investment insurance schemes. The D.A.C. has no multilateral funds for aid at its disposal.

The European Development Fund (E.D.F.) finances economic or social development schemes in the associated overseas countries by means of outright grants. The Fund has three particular features: it is a Community Fund; its action is supplementary; and it is democratically operated.

The regulations of the E.D.F. are simple. As far as is possible they avoid involving the associated overseas states in procedural complexities caused by unwieldy, exacting, and bureaucratic routine. It is the most easily administered fund in the world.

It will be understood that both Western organizations are at the present not well equipped to fulfill all the duties which are required to act as a single centralized organization dealing with all the aspects of Western aid and technical assistance.

Instead of discussing the shortcomings of both organizations I would like to give my ideas about the required Development Organization. First of all I wish to state that I am strongly in favour of a Free World Development Assistance Centre in which all advanced countries of the free world can take part and will operate very closely with the developing countries of the free world. As will be shown later on, I should like to see the developing countries take an active part in these development activities.

After describing the tasks which have to be fulfilled, I will show my proposed table of organization and the various branches. Centralized programming of aid and technical assistance is required. Not only is it necessary to set up sound development programmes for each developing country, but these programmes have to be attuned to each other in order to obtain also a harmonious development programme for the various regions and areas. Adequate staging of the national and area development programmes by qualified and experienced planners, familiar with the various local conditions is needed. Although we in the first place have to make use of Western experts, it is my firm belief that we should be able to make use of the university graduates of the developing countries. The latter will be most familiar with local conditions, religion, social structure, geographic and climatic circumstances, etc., which could hamper our development projects and programmes. In this way the people of the developing countries are taking an active part in the accomplishment of the great development task, but of additional advantage is also that we offer many university graduates of the underdeveloped countries for whom there are no suitable jobs available in their own country, a chance to use their acquired knowledge. Nor must we neglect the fact that this co-operation between the Western and the coloured people for common ends will make for a better understanding of the development programmes and projects. The branch dealing with the task mentioned above will be able to advise how to best use the multilateral funds made available, taking into account also the bilateral aid and technical assistance and the various foreign private investments in the developing world. The branch may advise also the member countries with regard to bilateral aid in order to prevent a

188

concentration of aid to some countries, but also to ensure that the bilateral aid fits in well with the development programmes. Until now there has been little sound programming of the education of the people of the various developing countries. Most nations are offering scholarships within their national aid programmes without taking into account whether the study concerned fits well into the needs of the developing country. Too often people in the educational field of the advanced nation that grants scholarships give their advice, but in my opinion that could better be done by economists and particularly by the people of this branch of the proposed Development Centre.

It will be understood that this programming branch will never be able to work without knowledge of all aid and technical assistance activities (multilateral, bilateral or on a private basis).

The second branch has for that reason to be charged with the collection and registration of all development activities, and also with the production of statistics. Furthermore this branch has to be informed about the progress of the development programmes. In order to be able to act really as a central agency of information about development activities an agreement has to be achieved whereby all nations concerned and all the existing multi-national organizations agree to keep this branch continuously well informed. The third branch has to be charged with the execution of the multilateral technical assistance in accordance with the development programmes, made up by the programming branch. One of the important duties will also be the most sincere selection of technical advisers, who will be sent out by this Development Centre. Furthermore it may work as a consultative body with regard to the national scientific institutes, which might be of great value both for the developing countries and the technical advisers. I stressed the importance of foreign private investment in the developing countries. The fourth branch could be charged in close co-operation with the first to advise in connexion with foreign investment possibilities in the developing countries and above all with the stimulation of foreign private investment. Governments and foreign private enterprise must be partners in progress for the benefit of each country, but in the past foreign private investors have too often been rudely treated.

Advice with regard to the treatment of foreign private capital for the developing countries might lead to a change in the attitude of the governments of those countries which are now avoided by foreign private capital. A substantial expansion of the flow of direct investment could be the result of adequate information and also by a more liberal attitude on the part of the developing countries. The foreign

189

investor will have a decided preference for countries which maintains law and order, effective management of the monetary and fiscal system designed to prevent both serious fluctuations in the value of money and crises in external payments. In my opinion a multi-national fund is required which is able to present a reasonable guarantee to the foreign private investor. Already some national governments have taken action in this direction. However, I think that within the framework of a multi-national development organization a guarantee-fund would be preferable, not only because it would stimulate foreign private investments to the side of smaller member countries, but also because this organization will be able to bring more pressure to bear upon the developing country, which is giving foreign private capital an unreasonably tough treatment. This guarantee fund can be established by the governments of member countries by means of loans. By a reasonable taxation of the foreign private enterprise which is having the benefit of this guarantee as a result of its contribution on a voluntary base, the fund may create its own working capital. I pointed out the need of an increase of inflow of capital in the developing countries and suggested foreign public loans for revenue-producing infrastructure projects such as railways, electric power stations and so on. In spite of the aid of the governments of the advanced countries, there exists still a considerable need for capital in order to accelerate the building up of infrastructure. I would like to suggest the creation of an investment fund for this purpose, built up by the participation of a large number of small private investors of all the advanced countries. As in the case of the suggested guarantee fund for foreign private investment, the governments of the member countries might give a start to this undertaking by giving an initial guarantee. I am sure that such an multi-national investment fund with an initial government guarantee, bearing a very low risk, will provide the required additional capital for revenue-producing infrastructure projects. If my suggestions could be realized, the task of this fifth branch must not be underestimated for it would greatly promote Western development diplomacy.

John Foster Dulles wrote in 1957, "There can never in the long run be real peace unless there is justice and law". Law performs an important function both in a community and in the world. Law is not a constant in a community (also in a world community), but a function. In all positive Law is hidden the element of power and that of interest. Law is not the same as power, nor is it the same as interest, but it gives expression to the former power relation.[63] All law presup-

63. Dr. B. V. A. Röling, International law in an expanded world, Amsterdam 1960, p. 15.

190

poses a community within which it is operative. What is needed today is a protective law with regard to foreign investment. Here, in this field, new international law that guarantees on one side political independence of a nation but on the other side the rights of private investment against discrimination or confiscation, is badly required, because it will stimulate foreign investment. As long as such a law does not exist, it is desirable to create a kind of advisory board, charged to give advice and, what is in my opinion more important, to achieve an agreement concerning legal rules accepted by the advanced countries and the developing nations with regard to foreign investment until a worldwide international law has come into being. It is desirable that the parties accept the jurisdiction of the International Court of Justice at the Hague in case of a difference of opinion about the legality of a measure taken by one of the parties. Hence, a sixth branch dealing with juridical affairs might be desirable.

The table of organization of the proposed Free World Development Centre could be in the main as follows:

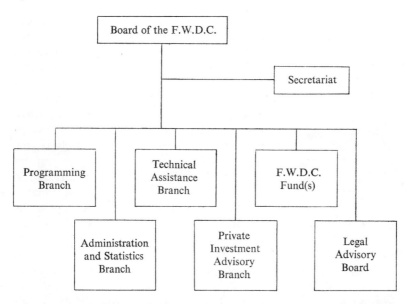

If it should be possible to transform the D.A.C. of the O.E.C.D. into an organization as described above, we would meet two ends. First, we are using an existing multi-national organization which most advanced nations have joined already and which has no direct relation with N.A.T.O. All members and associated countries of the O.E.C.D. belong to the free world and those non-Communist countries, which like to join the proposed F.W.D.C. of the O.E.C.D. are able to maintain neutrality if they want to and consequently need not fear becoming involved in the cold war or to be linked by a roundabout way with N.A.T.O.

Second, we are able to draw the representatives of the developing countries into the programming and other developing activities, which will result in a better co-operation and undoubtly in a better understanding of the development problems.

The question will now arise "What about the European Development Fund"? Has it to be abolished or has it to be linked with the proposed F.W.D.C. of the O.E.C.D.? I am not in favour of the abolition of the E.D.F., certainly for many years to come.

When the United Kingdom and other European nations have joined the E.E.C., this organization will represent a considerable economic power. The associated countries will have the benefit of the large European market to which they have access .On the other hand the links between Europe and both Asia and Africa are so tight as a result of economic co-operation in freedom, that it would be absolutely wrong to disturb this fruitful co-operation. The close links between European countries and developing nations result in an ever-increasing aid and technical assistance. The reciprocal interest and growing confidence should not be disturbed till the time for an Atlantic Economic Community with a larger number of associated countries becomes possible. The economic unification of Europe is of such a great value and is such a delicate political affair, that we have to prevent anything which could endanger its achievement. It is true that the European Development Fund is not equipped to perform all the development activities as we mentioned above with regard to the suggested F.W.D.C. of the O.E.C.D. However, in my opinion close co-operation between these two organizations will be possible. Exchange of information and a continuous reporting of all national and E.D.F. development activities, including foreign private enterprise in the developing countries to the O.E.C.D. will result in a much more efficient development policy and organization. The outcome may be also that more capital will flow to the developing countries and less money is wasted as a result of insufficiently co-ordinated development programmes.

Our final aim must be the integration of the E.D.F. and the proposed F. W. D. C. of the O.E.C.D., but this aim will require time, mainly on political grounds and furthermore will the re-organization be a time-consuming affair. Not to disturb the existing and short-term development plans in order to speed up the aid and technical assistance, we have to phase the melting together of the mentioned development organizations—the E.D.F. and the F.W.D.C.

N.A.T.O. has for the above-mentioned reasons an interest in the developing countries. N.A.T.O. may have a distinct preference for certain developing countries on political, economic or strategic grounds, as N.A.T.O. is not involved directly in the development activities, and consequently is not able to increase the aid and technical assistance to certain countries in order to accelerate their progress. However, when N.A.T.O. has expressed its preferences for the development of certain countries to the governments of the N.A.T.O. partners, the national authorities will be able to take adequate action.

As we have seen, the amount of bilateral aid and technical assistance surpasses the multilateral aid considerably and consequently there always exists a possibility to accelerate the economic development of one or more specific developing countries on military or strategic economic grounds, without interference in the distribution of multilateral aid, based on general sound development programmes. It will be understood that in such cases the multilateral aid and technical assistance should not be decreased taking into account the increased bilateral aid as a result of a N.A.T.O. recommendation. Therefore N.A.T.O. has no need to be included directly in the development policy. However, N.A.T.O. always will be in favour of a rapid economic development of the developing countries. Economic progress, a fair distribution of wealth and a rise in the level of education will alltogether promote political stability and consequently make the developing nations less vulnerable to Soviet influence and propaganda. From an organizational point of view there is thus no need to link N.A.T.O. with any multi-national development organization and all recommendations of N.A.T.O. for increased aid to any developing country will be brought about by the national authorities of the N.A.T.O. members.

CHAPTER X

CONCLUSION

When we disregard the facts of the world about us, disaster will follow. The world has been moving towards international organization and reciprocal economic dependence. Political changes immediately influence the state of affairs in our present world. Both the economies and the defensive power of the advanced countries of the Western world are affected by political changes in the developing world. When we declare solemnly that peace comes first as the Western countries' greatest interest, we are confused or hypocritical. The confusion involved here is that submission to the Communists should give us peace. The most passionate determination to avoid a total nuclear war will not by itself save us. One should remember, how during this century, nations and dictators have committed aggression which they had previously solemnly abjured. Despite a conscious and determined intention to avoid war, we may become involved in a frightening clash of arms. India, who liked to parade as a model of a definitely neutral peace-loving nation, attacked the Portuguese overseas province Goa although it always argued that controversies should be solved by discussion and not by force of arms.

Recently India was attacked by Communist China in spite of its (in all other cases) scrupulously maintained neutrality in the East-West controversy. President Nehru now has learned that peace based on powerless defence is likely to end in war.

What we in the West, in N.A.T.O. and in the free world want is security. The road to security and peace is to discover how we may defend the N.A.T.O. territory without war. A peace based on inadequate defence is likely to end in war. History has proved the correctness of this assertion. No one will resort to total war as an instrument of policy so long as there exists a nuclear deterrent on both sides. This means that N.A.T.O. must put the greatest emphasis for its defence, on the offensive strategic and tactical nuclear forces. History has shown that more often than not, the supreme commanders advised their governments— and in some cases dictators —not to wage war but to use the threat of existing military power to put pressure on the opposing power so that the political aim

194

could be achieved and the required concessions obtained. The more credible the Western nuclear threat becomes, the more the Communists will understand that war does not pay.

The credibility of the nuclear threat depends to a very large extent on the existence of an adequate command structure and a practically indestructible communications-system. It is realized too little that the value of the most sophisticated weapon system will be decreased if there is not also a practically infallible communications-system. The initial nuclear counter-attack is decisive, and the time needed to repeat the nuclear offensive missions. In modern air warfare time is of the highest value. The most important factor in a nuclear war is the size of destruction that can be achieved within a given time and an adequate communications-system is decisive for the number of nuclear missions that can be flown or the number of guided weapons with nuclear warheads that can be launched. The bigger the nuclear threat, the greater will be the risk an aggressor has to face. It is the knowledge that the country attacked will use maximum nuclear power in its counter-offensive and maximum destruction will be achieved in the shortest possible time, that will be the decisive factor in safeguarding peace. Recently the Cuba affair has proved the value of an overwhelming nuclear threat to force the opponent to moderate his aggressive attitude and to restore the status quo. The balance of nuclear capability of East and West is at the moment the most valuable peacemaker. The calculated risk in waging war is too great and the U.S.S.R. is well aware of that. For that reason the Communists are now trying to attain their political ends by other means. These means are of a political, psychological and economic nature and have as the object the weakening of our strength. We will not be able to pay for our defence and especially for our nuclear deterrent should the economies of the N.A.T.O. countries become undermined by the loss of foreign markets or lack of essential raw materials and tropical farm products. N.A.T.O. defence would also be endangered if strategically located countries of the free world became satellites of the U.S.S.R. The threat of the existing U.S. nuclear power has forced the U.S.S.R. to dismantle its military bases on Cuba. The task of military power is to prevent war and never to wage war. However, when war breaks out, it is the result of the disturbance in the balance of military power. The maintenance of adequate military power is the price we have to pay to safeguard peace and this price can never be too high compared to the miseries of war!

It can be argued that we are wasting our money by spending so much on defence, whilst millions of people in the underdeveloped countries go hungry. However, N.A.T.O. is forced to maintain an adequate defence as the principal political aim of the Communists is world domination.

The N.A.T.O. deterrent exists not only to deter the Communists from total war as an instrument of policy, but also to enable the West to take such political action, included defence measures, as may be required to protect ourselves. Further it gives the developing nations a fair chance and time to grow to maturity in freedom, without being forced to commit themselves to one of the two opposing blocs i.e. N.A.T.O. and the Communists.

Neither the N.A.T.O. countries nor the new nations of the developing world would like to lose their liberty and independence. N.A.T.O. is at present the only force in the free world able to guarantee liberty for all the peace-loving countries and to prevent the Communists from attaining their political ends. The existing N.A.T.O. forces are required to prevent Communist world domination.

The aim of N.A.T.O. and of the whole Western world is not only the prevention of Communist world domination. Our main aim is to create a world, in which there will be freedom, prosperity, co-operation and health for everybody. If the Western world had adopted a self-interested attitude, the aid and technical assistance would have been concentrated only on those developing nations of strategic importance or in the interest of Western prosperity. However, the people of the advanced countries are giving aid and technical assistance to all developing countries without any discrimination. The only stricture that can be passed on Western behaviour is that many associated developing nations sometimes receive more aid as a result of historical links with the former European countries. However, by the distribution of aid and technical assistance by the West as a whole this fact has been taken into account to a certain extent.

The United States of America are giving considerable aid to most of the developing nations which are not associated with Europe; therefore we cannot speak of a really harmonious distribution of aid.

There is no denying that the poor co-ordination of the development programmes of the various multi-national organizations and Western countries has sometimes resulted in discrepancies.

It is for that reason that I laid stress on a re-organization and a concentration of all development activities in order to promote a better distribution and use of Western aid.

The United Nations are unable to safeguard freedom in the world, because of the Communist frustration of the United Nations and its subordinate organizations and the lack of an adequate military power. As long as the political aim of the Communists is world-domination, they never can nor should be accepted as trustworthy defenders of freedom and self-determination. In the case of the revolt stemming from the wish for self-determination in Hungary, the United Nations were unable to take any adequate action, except a majority-declaration of disapproval of the Soviet military action.

In our present world N.A.T.O. is simply the sole power, able to prevent Communist world domination and to give the developing free nations a chance of undisturbed growth to political and economic maturity. Once the developing world has at its disposal the military power to defend its own interest and self-determination, N.A.T.O.'s task can be reduced to the self-defence of the Western Nations' territory. However, many decades will pass before the developing world is able to defend itself. Money spent to build up a military force in the developing world, would result in a serious retardation of the economic development as the building up of a military force requires not only capital but also skilled manpower and an adequate economic potential to support the military forces.

In view of the task N.A.T.O. has to accomplish, the national economies of the N.A.T.O. countries must be able to support the military forces. Defence is at present a very complicated affair. It requires a time-consuming and intensive basic and applied research as well as development. Furthermore a huge industrial potential, skilled manpower, energy, communications, raw materials and so on are required. The national economies must be able to bear the cost of defence. It should be well understood in this nuclear age that only existing military power makes real sense and can be used as a deterrent whereas forces which have to be mobilized have only a very relative value in time of peace because of the time that mobilization takes. The peace economies of the N.A.T.O. countries depend to a certain extent upon the acquisition of essential raw materials and trade with the developing countries. The growing economies of the advanced countries require an extension of the world market in order to safeguard full-employment and to obtain finance required for aid to the developing countries. On the other hand, to open and maintain markets for exports from the developing countries requires the advanced countries to pursue liberal trade policies.

I have described the problems we are facing in the development of the new nations in order to prove that it will take decades for the developing world to grow to political and economic maturity. Our development diplomacy should be organized in such a way that all our efforts (aid and technical assistance) bring in a maximum yield. This is not the case at present time. Too much effort is wasted because of poor co-ordination and poor staged development programmes, amateurism, inefficiency and so on.

As prosperity is the best promotor of peace, we in the West do our best to accelerate the economic growth within the developing world. In the history of mankind, economic strength and political power have influenced, in a fundamental way, the relationship between nations. With regard to the balance of political power, this has been governed largely by many factors other than economic. However, at present the economic factors are usually more important than political interests. Today it can be said that the wealth and productive power of the countries and regions of the earth have, more than ever in history, greatly effect the political balance.

With regard to racial discrimination I must stress that this is one of the worst evils in our human society, creating tensions which should be averted. It is true that the developing nations have suffered from racial discrimination, but it would be wrong, now that the rules are reversed, to prevent the creation of a multi-racial society and to threaten the white minorities in the developing countries, which can be of such a value to the development of the country. To promote reciprocal understanding and appreciation in order to achieve co-operation and prosperity in the free world, and thus world peace, migration and the creation of multi-racial societies have to be seen as the illuminating evidence of the endorsement of the principle of the United Nations Charter concerning equal human rights. In this Charter the people of the United Nations determined amongst other things to reaffirm faith in fundamental human rights, in the dignity and worth of the human person, in the equal rights of men and women, and to achieve these ends "to practice tolerance and live together in peace with one another as good neighbours". The people resolved to combine their efforts to accomplish these aims. Let us live according to the letter and the spirit of this testimony, to the benefit of all, regardless of the colour of their skin.

It is a fact that the most effective motivation for providing aid has very often been the desire to influence the recipients. It is still the main motivation of the Communists and the fact that the U.S.S.R. is giving aid only to selected countries, proves this. The developing nations also know that Soviet technical advisers (in 1961 more than 9,600 people) have tried to influence internal political affairs. Someone has made the following definition: "Diplomacy is the art of saying "nice doggy" until you have time to pick up a rock". Soviet diplomacy with regard to the developing countries is comparable with this definition and means giving aid until the developing country has become a satellite! As the Communists like to show themselves as the real and only benefactors of the underdeveloped countries, it may be interesting to cite what Khrushchev said during an interview with

Mr. Coles in 1961: "Communism is explained in such a way that when there is only one pair of trousers for ten persons and this pair of trousers is equally divided..., we all walk without trousers. We reject such a Communism without trousers". Altruïsm is alien to the Communist leader. The Soviet system of extending aid is almost exclusively in the form of soft loans, instead of grants, usually repayable in local currency over a period of 10 to 12 years. However, Western aid is for a large part in the form of grants (see Appendix). The total number of grants and public loans is considerable and Soviet aid is insignificant compared to Western aid. As well as Western public aid, is the amount of Western private investment also of great value to the developing countries. Western aid to the developing countries must not be seen as a policy to link the newly independent nations to N.A.T.O. Firstly, N.A.T.O. is not a supranational government and therefore not comparable with the Soviet government and secondly N.A.T.O. has no development fund at its disposal.

As I explained at the outset, our peace making task depends to a large extent on the economic co-operation of the developing countries. We respect their independence and do not want them to become our satellites! As prosperity is the best promotor of peace we do our best to accelerate their growth to economic maturity which leads eventually to political maturity. Historic and economic factors have created narrow ties between advanced and developing countries. When the colonial period came practically to an end, it did not mean that the former colonial powers had let them down. On the contrary, the aid given to the new nations increased enormously. The new political structure of the free world is promoting peace and political stability.

The widely-circulated idea that the contest between East and West will be decided in the "third world" ("the developing world") is wrong. The main struggle between East and West in the political, psychological and economic sense, takes place directly between the two opposing blocs, as the "balance of nuclear terror" is founded on the military power of the blocs. N.A.T.O. defence only aimed at preventing the developing world from getting directly involved in the East-West controversy and becoming the political playground of the advanced countries!

We cannot neglect the fact that the economies of the European countries have a large interest in the development of Latin America, Africa and the free Asiatic countries. The United States economy is closely linked with Latin America. For that reason it is understandable that Europe and the U.S.A. are especially interested in the development of those parts of the free world, which are of vital importance

199

to their respective peace-economies. It should be understood by the U.S.A. that there are circumstances forcing them into a development policy, which is different from the general pattern. Anti-colonial obsession is dogging and bedevilling United States' relations and co-operation with one of the most loyal and valuable allies, notably Portugal. There is a great difference between the white colonists not mixing with the native population and miscegenation taking place. In the latter case a multi-racial community is created in the Portuguese provinces as a result of the laudable attitude of the Portuguese people towards coloured citizens. The Americans may take an example from the Portuguese attitude. A comparison between the construction and improvement of railways—there are about 2,900 kilometres in Angola and about 2,000 in Mozambique or the increase in energy potential —and the situation in the African developing countries, shows the value of Portuguese development activities. We are aiming at co-operation in the free world and in the case of the Portuguese overseas provinces, the U.S.A. simply tries to disorganize this community and to sow dissension. This policy may be due to unfamiliarity with the situation or a desire to please the people of African countries. Moreover, if Portugal loses its overseas provinces and this multi-racial community breaks down, unemployment would follow financial collapse, and transform Portugal into a Soviet base and satellite! It would also result in the loss of the strategically important Azores.

In my opinion loyalty to this N.A.T.O. partner is required and the future will definitely show that the multi-racial communities in the Portuguese overseas provinces are viable and will prove to be an illuminating example of interracial co-operation. This is the interracial co-operation which I have proposed within the framework of the suggested Free World Development Centre, forming part of the O.E.C.D. Interracial co-operation between European countries and the overseas associated countries, is very successful and no coloured student or representative of a developing country has obtained any impression of racial discrimination in Europe. I hope that the time will come when the E.E.C. Development Fund will grow into the proposed F.W.D.C. of the O.E.C.D. and that we shall be able to allow the coloured people of the developing countries to take over many of the functions in these development organizations. A statement of Kristensen should be mentioned: "The conclusion of all this is simple: one of the most important contributions which the major industrial countries can make to the sound economic development of the less advanced nations is to keep up as high and steady as possible the long-term rate of growth of their own economies. Needless to explain that this is also the only practicable policy for mobilizing the considerable volume of capital exports that should be chanelled to the underdeveloped regions, a policy which would at the same time satisfy industrial countries' internal needs for higher living standards and also facilitate the transformation required in their own economic structures."[64]

In previous chapters I have criticized facts, organizations and attitudes of certain governments, even the activities of our most important N.A.T.O. partner. It is not necessary to point out the enormous efforts of the United States of America with respect to both aid (or technical assistance) and the reinforcement of N.A.T.O.'s strength. Western Europe is well aware of the importance of the U.S.A. for its existence and freedom as well as for the development of the new countries. However, the purpose of my criticism was to show existing shortcomings and the necessity for a better understanding of Western Europe's attitude to various political problems, based on centuries old experience. I do not think that there is any sense in explaining mistakes away. The purpose of this study is only to improve the Western defence and the development in freedom of the new countries as well as to further understanding, reciprocal respect and above all co-operation between all races in the free world.

Political planning must be aware of military realities, and military plans in turn must be responsive to political considerations. Political considerations have to take into account economic interests. The economic interdependence in the free world is growing and this will definitely be to the benefit of the developing countries.

The logical consequence of these inter-relations is that we have to pay full attention to the strategic situation. Spain and Portugal hold important strategic positions within the over-all N.A.T.O. context. Likewise Turkey and Greece are of great value for the strategic position of N.A.T.O. and it is incomprehensible that the other N.A.T.O. countries give considerable aid and technical assistance to the developing countries, as important as this is, but are not doing their utmost to accelerate the economic growth of these partners! Independent North Africa also holds an important strategic position and for that reason the political attitude of North Africa is of vital interest to N.A.T.O. with regard to our position in the Mediterranean. The Middle East and some parts of Asia are important for the defence of Europe. The development of all these countries is important for Europe, just as the development of Latin America is in the interest of the Western Hemisphere. Our Western aid programmes have to be aimed at a rapid increase of prosperity in all these countries in

64. T. Kristensen, Economic development and international co-operation; Series on lectures on economic growth O.E.C.D. publication, Paris, 1961.

order to keep communism away. All in all, we want political stability and prosperity especially in all countries which are located in areas that are of decisive importance to N.A.T.O.

Military forces today do not exist to wage war; their purpose is to prevent it. N.A.T.O.'s task is to guarantee political and economic development in freedom and without pressure from outside on the developing countries. The natural resources and the growing markets of the developing countries are strengthening the economies of N.A.T.O. countries and consequently enabling the Western countries to maintain an adequate defence.

There are no links between N.A.T.O. and the developing countries and we do not want to commit themselves to the West.

The most important aim of N.A.T.O. and the justification of its existence has a distinctly positive character. The main object of N.A.T.O. is to safeguard the self-determination of all the peoples in the free world, regardless of whether they belong to an advanced or a developing country.

Finally, what happens in the developing countries is of vital importance to N.A.T.O. and N.A.T.O. is of vital importance to them in their growth to maturity in a free world. This is the important relation between the "Developing Countries" and "N.A.T.O.".

EXPLANATORY LIST OF ABBREVIATIONS

E.C.A.	Economic Commission for Africa.
E.C.A.F.E.	Economic Commission for Asia and for the Far East.
E.C.L.A.	Economic Commission for Latin America.
E.C.O.S.O.C.	Economic and Social Council of the U.N.
F.A.O.	Food and Agriculture Organization of the U.N.
I.A.E.A.	International Atomic Energy Agency.
I.B.R.D.	International Bank for Reconstruction and Development.
I.C.A.O.	International Civil Aviation Organization.
I.D.A.	International Development Association.
I.F.C.	International Finance Corporation.
I.L.O.	International Labour Organization.
I.T.U.	International Telecommunication Union.
T.A.B.	Technical Assistance Board.
T.A.C.	Technical Assistance Committee.
S.F.	Special Fund of the U.N.
U.N.E.S.C.O.	United Nations Educational, Scientific and Cultural Organization.
U.N.I.C.E.F.	United Nations Children's Fund.
U.N.R.W.A.	United Nations Relief and Works Agency.
U.N.T.A.A.	United Nations Technical Assistance Administration.
U.N.E.P.T.A.	United Nations Expanded Programme of Technical Assistance.

LIST OF TABLES AND FIGURES

INDEX